The title of the original:

Sluta älta och grubbla – lättare gjort med kognitiv beteendeterapi.
Translated by Robert Bergman Carter

Olle Wadström
First edition 2007
Second edition 2009
Third edition 2011
Fourth edition 2014
English edition 2015

Graphic design and illustrations:
Lars-Åke Pettersson

Cover picture: Shutterstock

ISBN-13: 978-1511549776

© Psykologinsats

This work is protected by copyright. Reproduction is prohibited. Anyone who violates the copyright law can be prosecuted and sentenced to a fine or imprisonment, as well as being required to pay compensation to the author.

Quit Ruminating and Brooding

It is easier to do with Cognitive Behavior Therapy (CBT)

*How ruminating and brooding work
and what to do to overcome them*

Olle Wadström

Table of Contents

Preface 6

INTRODUCTION – before you start reading 8
    A book on ruminations – Why?. 8
    How do you read this book? 9

RUMINATIONS AND BROODINGS – a very common human behavior 11
    What is ruminating? 11
        When do we ruminate? 11
    Everyday ruminations 12
        Ruminations in daily life 12
        Ruminations in various states of anxiety 14
    Ruminating in Obsessive Compulsive Disorder 14
    Ruminating in social anxiety disorder 15

WHAT ARE RUMINATIONS AND BROODINGS? 17
    Rumination is a behavioral stream 18
        Thoughts that frighten and lead to discomfort – thoughts that calm and comfort 18
        Thoughts that worry – discomforting thoughts. 18
        Calming thoughts – comforting thoughts. 20
        Ruminating is the tennis of the brain – the internal arguing 22
    What drives ruminations and broodings? 24
        Reinforcement. 24
        Premack's principle 25
        Ruminating is a chain of thoughts 26
        Conditioning – how you can become afraid of your own thoughts. 28
        Generalization. 30
        You get dumber during anxiety 31
    Summary. 32

CURE THE RUMINATIONS 33
    Exposure with response prevention 35
    Learn to recognize comforting thoughts 38
    Different types of comforting thoughts. 42
    A case with manipulating of history. 45
    Ruminating can cease spontaneously 46
    The serenity prayer. 47
    Is it always wrong to fight thoughts that lead to anxiety and doubt? 47
    Establishing circumstances 48
    Do not think positive. 51

A few resources and "tricks" to do the right things in treatment 52
    Acceptance 52
    The technique of thinking "the worst thought" 54
    Beware of alternative thoughts 56
    Logic and reason are meaningless 57
    Do not try to understand why 57
    Mindfulness – to be present in the moment 58
    Cognitive defusion 59
    Harmful behavior or behavior in disharmony with the treatment of ruminations 61
    A particularly puzzling case 62
    Fatalism 64
What happens to ruminations during behavior therapy 65
    Stop the ruminating right from the start 68
    A summary of techniques or tools for counteracting comforting thoughts 69

WHEN RUMINATIONS WILL NOT QUIT 72

RUMINATIONS IN CASES OF OCD, JEALOUSY, HYPOCHONDRIA, AND SOCIAL PHOBIA
Ruminating in OCD 74
    Summary of advice to grip with rumination in cases of OCD 79
Ruminations in social phobia 81
Harmony in OCD and social phobia 83

RELIGIOUS BROODINGS 85

DECISION-ANXIETY 86
    The big decision 90
    Treatment of decision-anxiety 91

ANTICIPATORY ANXIETY 92
    Being afraid of your thoughts 94
    How do you prevent expectation anxiety? 95
    Treatment of expectation anxiety 96

CLOSING WORDS 100
    Reference for the scientific base of this book 101

Appendix A. *Are you a ruminator and a brooder?* 103

Appendix B. *General advice and approaches for you who wish to get rid of ruminations and broodings, and have less anxiety in the long term* 106

Appendix C. *E-mail correspondence with a ruminating patient* 108

Glossary 120

PREFACE

To Thinking Janne

It is not common among people who call themselves behavioral analysts or behavioral therapists to attempt a behavioral analysis of cognitive behaviors. One likely reason for this is that thoughts (cognitions) are internal and cannot be measured or observed in the same way as external, motor behaviors. Demands for visibly measurable results of the treatment cannot, in these cases, be met. When working with behavioral analysis, this demand is close to holy.

I do not feel that it is reason enough to not attempt to understand and find ways to treat a thought-behavior such as rumination. Whatever the case, many – maybe even most of us – suffer from ruminations and broodings. Both of these lead to anxiety, concerns and sleepless nights. Rumination and brooding are significant components of compulsive disorders and social anxiety disorders, and can in these cases not be ignored. In these cases, there must be some way to approach them.

Another reason to dedicate oneself to the problem of rumination is that it is a willfully controllable behavior, even if the ruminator does not always experience it in that way. Rumination is a learned behavior such as any other motor behavior. Treatments that are based on learning, such as CBT, should for this reason be interested in rumination. Difficulties of "touching the behavior" should therefore not lead to not handling it. One way to make rumination more substantial is by looking at it as "self-talk".

Considering how much suffering it brings, and how much private time that is spent doing it, I see it as an urgent matter to teach a way of tackling it based on behavioristic premises. This book describes how behavior therapy can be used to treat a cognitive behavior.

Preface

This book is an attempt to provide an approach to the behaviors of ruminating and brooding. It can be applied whether the ruminating is of an everyday character or if it is part of a more serious condition. It is my ambition that the reader will understand, not only how to face his or her ruminating, but also why he or she should act in the manner described.

Visit http://psykologinsats.se/files/files/PDF/Rumination2013_olle.pdf for the scientific base of this book or search on the internet for "When Mowrer is not enough".

Linköping, June 2007

Olle Wadström

INTRODUCTION

Before you start reading
If you suffer from ruminations and brooding, which you intend to do something about, I suggest that you start by completing the questionnaire in Appendix A. and take note of your score. I also recommend that you continuously, on a daily basis at the same time of day, summarize the approximate number of minutes of the day that you have spent ruminating, and write this down.

Just by reading this book, your approach to ruminating will be changed, and through this – so will your ruminating. It is likely that your ruminating will decrease even before you have actively decided on doing something. If you then decide on working more actively, changes will be apparent in both your registered minutes as well as your score on the questionnaire in Appendix A. when you complete it again. Continuously follow the developments of your ruminating by registering minutes spent ruminating and through the questionnaire in Appendix A.

By measuring your ruminating you will get feedback on your progress. If progress does not occur, you can do an analysis in order to find out why this is.

A book on ruminations – Why?
To my knowledge, there have been no previous behavioral analyses of rumination and brooding which have resulted in a conscious and clearly described strategy for treatment. I have taken the challenge to explain what keeps ruminating going, despite the fact that people claim that ruminating makes them feel bad, and that they want to be rid of it.

I have tested the methodology which was the result of my analysis on both my own patients as well as on my friends who had everyday ruminations. They claim that it has been helpful. They have also stated that the analysis makes ruminating more understandable, and that they can now understand why they have not been able to give it up earlier. The method which I suggest is not a new one, but rather an application of well-proven behavior therapy methods with scientific support. The exciting part is the application to ruminating – a cognitive (thought-) behavior.

My hopes are that this book will be able to help everyone who is ruminating and brooding to rid themselves of this self-torture. I have aimed at making this book simple and straight forward, so that it can be read and understood by the general public, but I hope that behavior therapists (Cognitive behavior therapists) and other therapists will embrace it as well. The content is wholly based on behavior analysis and principles of learning-psychology.

How do you read this book?

This book consists of two sections; one general section and one that presents examples of serious rumination, as it is in cases where the duration of anxiety is longer and more painful, as in cases of anxiety disorder.

The general section covers all types of rumination and ruminating, both everyday ruminations as well as more serious cases. In this section, I describe what it looks like and what drives it, as well as how to come to terms with it. This general section is on pages 6-73, and is the core of this book, and should be read by all, as well as pages 85-119.

The second section presents examples from difficult and painful rumination, and is presented on pages 74-84. The examples in this section are from cases of anxiety disorders, Obsessive Compulsive Disorder, Social Anxiety Disorder, but also hypochondria, and jealousy, and can be read by everyone, even those who feel that they only suffer from everyday ruminating.

My ambition has been to provide numerous examples from my clinical, as well as my everyday experiences. There are, in general, not any differences between ruminations and brooding, despite context and personality. This means that certain details will appear in several places in this book. Those who choose to read the whole book will recognize and see similarities in different cases. These repetitions are not a case of ruminating on my behalf, rather, they are a result of my using case descriptions with different backgrounds and severity. Rumination in itself always looks the same, no matter how severe it is.

Rumination is such a difficult problem to treat that I recommend everyone to read this book from beginning to end, even if this means reading several similar cases, and despite the fact that the examples provided may not seem to be of the same severity as your own situation.

Rumination is always rumination. And even if your own ruminations and broodings are not that severe, there is still much to be gained from understanding and knowing about more severe forms. It is hereby possible to learn how to handle it, and in this way, avoid developing it into a more severe problem.

At the end of the book are several appendices. There is a questionnaire, a glossary with explanations for words that can be hard to understand the first time you encounter them in this text.

RUMINATIONS AND BROODINGS
– a very common human behavior

Apart from humans, no other living creature has the ability to think about things in ways that lead to ruminations and brooding. Ruminations are probably the psychological "scourge" that most people suffer from. Not just patients who seek help for it, but all of us. Anyone can sometimes be afflicted by ruminating about things that nothing can be done about. We are tormented by ruminations when we lie sleepless at night, we are tormented by them when we are alone, or whenever we have parts of our thinking free for use. We are tormented by them for hours, days, and even years, now and then during our entire lives.

What is ruminating?
Ruminations are thoughts. Thoughts are a type of behavior, so called cognitive behavior. Other types of behavior are motor or external behaviors. These behaviors are what we do with our bodies and which are usually visible, while cognitive behaviors occur inside of us and are not directly observable. Autonomous behavior, a third kind of behavior, differs from the external/motor and cognitive behavior in that it cannot be controlled by will, and it is run by an independent nervous system – the autonomous nervous system. Autonomous behavior includes things that happen in our bodies, often without us knowing about them, for example, our heart beat, our blood vessels expanding, sweating, our stomachs processing food and our intestines absorbing nourishment etc. Autonomous behavior includes what happens in our body when we get angry, scared, or excited.

> We have three types of behavior. These are external/motor behavior, cognitive/thought-behavior and autonomous/emotional behavior.

When do we ruminate
Rumination is something we have access to whenever and wherever during our waking time. As long as we have a functional brain, it is possible to ruminate. Typically, we ruminate during situations where uncertainty, doubt and hesitation

are involved. Rumination is usually an attempt to solve both solvable as well as unsolvable problems in our minds. It is often about making real decisions, but since we lack sufficient information about the future, no real decisions can be made. "Should I accept the job I was offered, or..." "Is he really the right one for me" " I wonder if something bad will happen to me if I go to the U.S.A.?" Rumination is often a pointless attempt to seek answers to questions that have no certain answers. It can also be a way to protect oneself from real or unreal threats.

It is also common to ruminate and brood over things that have already happened, and attempt to sort out things that cannot be sorted out. "Why did I say no to that job that I was offered?" "Why did I break up with Stina, if I hadn't done that, she wouldn't be married to Stellan now."

There is also ruminating connected to situations involving choices or decisions. You ruminate on how to decide before making the decision, and afterwards you ruminate on whether or not you made the right decision. Ruminations in decision-situations are often referred to as "decision-anxiety".

We also ruminate about things that are too embarrassing to ask about, or things we do not dare to ask about. "I wonder if they noticed that I sat silent all night." "I wonder if they'll notice that I'm nervous." Rumination can also be a way to prepare for a difficult and worrying situation, or to go through events in hindsight to find out if you embarrassed yourself or how you were perceived by others. Since you do not want to get any attention by asking, you ruminate instead.

> Ruminating is a chain of behaviors (thoughts) that we use to try to bring clarity, convince ourselves, prepare ourselves for, or ensure ourselves of something, but where we cannot achieve the certainty we want to achieve.

Everyday ruminations

Ruminations in daily life

We have gotten our thinking ability, for better or worse. When humankind lived in forests where wild animals were a constant threat, it was advantageous for our survival to be able to recognize dangers before they became real or close. It was important to have the imagination to visualize a bear behind a big rock, and accordingly to take a detour in order to have a head start, and get away from the bear. It was important to realize dangers ahead of time in order to be able to avoid them.

People who had a vivid imagination and the ability to foresee and imagine dangers before they were apparent and real, had better chances for survival. As long as there was a realization that a situation might be dangerous, there was a possibility to devise protective measures and strategies. Awareness and the ability to imagine dangers made it possible to make use of safety behavior. The ability to conceive of and to predict dangers can be seen as a life-saving cognitive activity in Stone Age humans. Early humankind needed ruminating for its survival. The need for this type of cognitive activity is not as necessary in our times.

We are now living in a world where ruminating is not life-saving in the same way. Our brains, that have evolved to become imaginative, will accordingly make us see dangers that do not exist in our relatively harmless world. We are afflicted by unnecessary, discomforting thoughts that warn us of dangers that are not real dangers. However, since we are in completely different contexts than Stone Age humans, our brains come up with completely different dangers.

We worry about if we will not get the job we applied for, and if we don't, what will we do? We ponder over what our work colleagues say about us and what we can do to find out, and eventually change what they say. Our thoughts are occupied with what we should do if our washing-machine breaks down, since we do not have enough money to instantly replace it with a new one. We can even ponder over if what we said to Lisa made her sad, and what we in that case can say to her to make her happy. We brood on whether or not there is a life after this one, and if we are living our lives the way we were supposed to. We ponder over the big questions of life, is there a God? what is the meaning of life?

Our ruminations occur in different situations, and often in connection to feelings of worry and anxiety. Ruminations can have different names, depending on the context in which they appear. Sometimes they are referred to as guilty conscience, sometimes as anticipatory anxiety, decision-anxiety in other contexts, and with a different content they can be referred to as religious broodings or a crisis of life. It is the same type of activity going on in our brains, only the content of our thoughts varies. The function of this thinking is always the same, as we try to solve problems with our cognitive behavior. Sometimes the problems are impossible to solve, or they can only be solved through exterior behaviors. But often, ruminating is about trying to solve unsolvable problems in our minds.

Ruminating in various types of anxiety

Nearly every human being has been ruminating. The everyday ruminating that we do does not distinguish itself in terms of characteristics from the ruminating and brooding that are parts of a more serious state of anxiety. The difference is that everyday rumination is not as persistent and longstanding, and it is not as painful. There are a few anxiety disorders that are known to be characterized by persistent rumination and brooding. The most common ones are Obsessive Compulsive Disorder, jealousy, hypochondria, Social Anxiety Disorder, and generalized anxiety disorder.

In cases of these anxiety disorders, ruminating is a major part of the problem. In some cases it is the dominant and most painful behavior for the patient. Ruminating is often a way to try to convince oneself, to calm oneself, to experience clarity and assurance and to finally feel better.

Ruminating in Obsessive Compulsive Disorder

Ruminating is an invisible compulsive behavior, which in combination with controlling, avoidance, and reassuring questions, make up what we call compulsive behavior. Ruminating in this case is like posing reassuring questions to oneself, and then attempting to answer them. It is sometimes claimed that ruminating is the compulsive behavior that is the most difficult to successfully treat. Some patients with OCD claim that their entire waking time is spent ruminating.

Just as other compulsive behavior cases in OCD, the ruminating aims at reducing doubt, insecurity and worries, or anxiety. Ruminating is self-convincing or self-persuasive (it is similar to the reassuring questions, but with the difference that in cases of rumination, the reassuring questions are directed towards oneself and even the answers are given by oneself).

Karin was working at a check-in counter at an airport. Once after a departure, she discovered a package the size of a football that had been left behind due to her negligence. This gave her great anxiety, and she was convinced that there was something important in the package. She made sure that the package would be sent as soon as possible to its destination, a hospital.

In spite of this, she could not stop thinking about the package. She believed that it contained something very important and that she might have caused harm by forgetting it. The thought that it might have contained a new heart for a heart-patient waiting for operation came up. This thought was so frightening that she did not dare to utter it to anyone. She did not dare to make any inquiries or to do anything that might raise attention. And she definitely did not dare speak to her manager. Perhaps she had killed someone? No, there was no chance that a heart would be sent by regular flight? Why not? The heart would be damaged by heat during the transport. But then again, there are clever ways to keep transplants cold, so it might be possible. And so, the ruminations and broodings had started.

Karin kept this ruminating up for more than a year, without being able to solve the problem. She contacted a therapist, to whom she after some doubts, told about her problem. The therapist reassured and comforted her by saying that naturally, there could not have been a heart in the package. It felt good to hear this, but in the next second, a new discomforting thought came to her: There is no way that the therapist can know this! The therapist's reassurances just worried her more, and she kept on brooding.

The ruminating seemed to be never ending and never gave her the peace, assurance and certainty that Karin wanted with her ruminating.

Ruminating in Social Anxiety Disorder

With a person with Social Anxiety Disorder, ruminating is often a mental preparation for a social situation which is feared and which is potentially humiliating. Ponderings and broodings on how things will go, what to say and what to do if something turns out to be embarrassing.

After a painful and distressing situation, ruminating can consist of, in one's ruminations doing a recap of what transpired, and how things went. What really happened, and how did people react to my behavior? Was I perceived as weak or ridiculous?

RUMINATING IN SOCIAL ANXIETY DISORDER

Jonas is pondering (ruminating) on how to act at the next meeting at his job. Since he is a team leader, he needs to talk quite a bit. This is inevitable. If he blushes, he can say that he needs to make a phone call and quickly leave the room.

After the meeting, he ruminates on how he managed the meeting. Did they see me blushing? Are they laughing at me? Am I a silly boss? Will they lose their respect for me now? He tries to find arguments for things not having been that bad. He ruminates on the meeting beforehand as well as afterwards, and suffers from it both before the meeting as well as afterwards.

Broodings around a small and meaningless meeting can go on for days, reappear and occupy and torment him for nights in his loneliness.

- Nisse probably thinks that I am a complete idiot? I didn't ask any questions. But neither did Bosse, and he's smart... but...

- Did they think that my presentation was completely worthless? But Anna looked interested. But Bosse seemed to be very skeptical... but...

16

WHAT ARE RUMINATION AND BROODING?

Ruminating is thought-behaviors – cognitive behaviors. The typical rumination is a type of internal struggle, an internal discussion where a person in his or her mind considers the possibilities to affect, alter, predict, understand, and prepare for something. Sometimes the problem being ruminated upon is not solvable through either thoughts or actions.

It is possible to control and affect thoughts, something that might be hard to believe for someone who suffers from a lot of ruminating. It feels as if you cannot quit ruminating, even if you really want to. Ruminating has a tendency to return, time and again. Yet the fact remains that we can control both our external actions (the motor behavior) as well as our thoughts (the cognitive behavior). The difference between controlling our actions and controlling our thought can be described accordingly.

We can decide between raising our right arm or not moving it at all. We can decide between speaking or being silent. Motor behaviors are under our absolute control, with the exceptions of reflexes and tics.

When it comes to thinking, the situation is slightly different. We can decide on thinking about a certain thing, **but** we cannot decide on not thinking at all. However hard we try, we will always be thinking about something. Thus, we cannot restrain ourselves from thinking in the same manner that we can restrain ourselves from moving. This is one of the problems with ruminating. We think during all of our waking time. It is also hard to not think about a certain thing, since we are constantly thinking, and it is easy to skip from one thought to another.

It has been proven difficult – indeed impossible – to decide on *not* thinking on, for example "a blue elephant". Indeed, as soon as you try to not think about the blue elephant, a blue elephant appears. This is because when you try to keep track of what to not think about, you automatically think about it.

Rumination is a behavior stream

Ruminating is not really one behavior, but rather a stream of many behaviors. It is a stream of thoughts. The rumination-stream does not consist of the same thoughts repeating themselves, but rather it consists of two types of thoughts. Two types which each have their own different function.

Behavior analysis is the understanding of the function of different behaviors. One behavior can have different functions, depending on different situations. Different behaviors may have the same function, even though they differ starkly. In order to understand a behavior's function or purpose, it is essential to see it its context. If you do not understand the function of a behavior, you might treat it improperly. Thoughts are also behaviors, which can have different functions.

Our feelings are affected by external and internal factors. We might get upset, angry, and frightened by things that we hear and see, but also by things that we think. In the same manner, we can be calmed by things we see, hear, and think.

Thoughts can frighten and lead to discomfort, thoughts can calm and comfort

Thoughts in ruminations have two different functions. One kind of thoughts leads to anxiety, insecurity, or discomfort and these thoughts function as frighteners or "triggers". The other type of thoughts functions as calmers, reassurers, or comforters, also called safety-behaviors.

Thoughts that lead to concern, frighten, lead to uneasiness, anxiety or discomfort in general will henceforth be referred to as *"discomforting thoughts"*. Thoughts that function as safety-behaviors that are used to rid uncertainty, insecurity, concerns, feelings of discomfort and doubt, will henceforth be referred to as *"comforting thoughts"*.

Thoughts that evoke anxiety discomforting thoughts
Discomforting thoughts can have varying appearances and contents. They can evoke discomfort by frightening and worrying us, they can lead to anxiety, irritate, provoke, confound us, make us insecure, and they can make us feel hurt, wronged or

insulted. Many people think in terms of images or scenarios, which does not make any difference for our line of reasoning.

The thoughts that evoke discomfort can have many different types of content. Their common denominator is that they evoke uneasiness and discomfort, more or less automatically. In the case of OCD, discomforting thoughts are also referred to as "emotion-thoughts".

Below are a few examples of discomforting thoughts:

Catastrophic thoughts

What if I fail my exam!
Am I going insane?
Mother might die.
I am surely going to get fired now.
The kids might get hit by a car when they are walking to school.
What was that look that she gave to Nisse when I protested?
What if I have cancer?
Does he mind me speaking, since he looked at me that way?
They can tell that I am nervous.
What if I do not find anyone to share my life with?

Doubt and insecurity thoughts

I wonder what he meant by asking *me* about this?
Did I hit someone when I was driving in the dark?
Was she sneering at me when I was speaking?
What if I forgot to lock the door?
Did I do the wrong thing when I...?
Does he not love me anymore?

Existential insecurity

What is the meaning of life?
Is there a God?
Has my life been in vain?
Will life never be more than this?
What happens after death?
Am I wasting my life?

Self-accusation thoughts
   Maybe I hurt her when I said that I did not want to?
   They probably did not understand what I meant. What if something goes wrong because of me, and they get hurt?
   Did he really understand what I meant?
   What if she thought that I was negative and criticizing when I said...?
   I wonder if he resented that?
   Is Pelle sad because I said that?
   How could I be so stupid that I...?
   I am a bad mother and I do not have time for the things I need to do at work either.

Comparing thoughts (along with jealousy thoughts)
   Which car is the best, and which one should I choose?
   Should I really get a new job?
   They probably just think that I am a dork. They despise me.
   I am not as good as they are.
   She does not love me as much as I love her.
   She is always better than me.
   I am always the worst.
   He is much smarter than me.
   Other people always get the best, while I always get the worst.
   Why is he just looking at her?

   A characteristic of the discomforting thoughts is that they trigger a feeling of worry, uneasiness, doubt, or some other unpleasant feeling.

Calming thoughts comforting thoughts

The other type, the comforting thoughts calm, reassure, and provide clarity, certainty or comfort. In terms of content and function they are the opposite of discomforting thoughts. They temporarily decrease the amount of discomfort. Rather than frightening, these thoughts are used to find explanations, solutions, remedies, and counteractions to the danger, convincing evidence or ways out of the situation. These thoughts are pleasant and provide comfort.

Comforting thought belong to the category of behaviors referred to as "safety behaviors". Safety behaviors are the behaviors which make us momentarily feel ease and comfort. Comforting thoughts are invisible safety behaviors which at least give a temporary pleasant and calming feeling.

A few examples of thoughts that comfort with calm, explanations and assuredness
- If I did have cancer, the doctor would have noticed it at my last check-up.
- Doctors are good at detecting cancer in people, so I can be calm.
- I have passed all the previous exams, so why would I not pass this one?
- I am not the biggest idiot in the group. Jocke often screws up.
- He probably asked me about that because I knew something similar the last time we talked, not because I looked strange.
- She probably likes me.
- The boss did not look my way when he was complaining. Was that really a sneer? She was smiling at Kalle as well.
- Nobody else gets AIDS from the door handle, so it should be safe for me as well.
- Of course he loves me and the children otherwise he would have left us…
- But I have never hit anyone with the car before, so why would I do it now?
- The meaning of life is to serve God.
- If I were going insane I would not be thinking like this. Those who are really insane do not realize it.
- If I did hit anyone with my car, other drivers would have noticed the victim and taken them to a hospital.
- Of course I am a good mother and worker, but everyone has a hard time making everything work all the time.
- I never did anything to him, so why should he be mad at me?

A characteristic of comforting thoughts is that they always provide some comfort and some calm. The calming thoughts can be logical, but they can also be unrealistic fantasies and pure wishful thinking. You think about how things might go or how they could have went. They can be fantasies of sort, or daydreams that give some temporary feelings of well-being in a situation that is perhaps hopeless or unsolvable.

- I hope that mean idiot dies.
- They will soon find out what type of person he is, and then they will regret

not giving that job to me.
– If I win a million, then I will…

A characteristic of comforting thoughts is that they at least give some temporary comfort or feel somewhat calming at the moment.

Ruminating is the "tennis" of the brain – the internal argumentation

Ruminations can be likened to a game of tennis, where one side hits a frightening thought, and the calming side returns it with a comforting thought. Each time the "ball" comes over to the other side, it can be returned. The game can go on forever. Since we are intelligent beings, we keep finding new frightening aspects, or we get new irritating ideas, and find new comforting thoughts.

Ruminating is an internal dialogue, or discussion or debate.

Our ability to see new dangers leads to a never ending shift in the contents of ruminations, even if it is about the same subject or field.

Look at this example of how rumination can function. Let the tennis game begin.

Discomforting thoughts

Comforting thoughts

1. What if the interest rate increases?

2. The interest rate has not increased for a year.

3. Sooner or later it is bound to increase. It has always been up and down. If it increases, our living costs will hit the ceiling and we will have to move.

4. No expert has talked about increased interest rates recently.

5. In the thirties, the stock market crashed and interest rates increased overnight without people knowing about it ahead of time, because

if they did, they would have sold their stock
shares before the crash.

> 6. Economists are more competent now, so that could not happen in such a surprising way these days.

7. But the monetary system is also more complicated now and, hence, more vulnerable. And if the interest rate increased by 2%, we might not be able to afford food. Then we will be forced to sell our house.

> 8. We will be alright, one way or another. We will get plenty of money for our house if we sold it now.

9. Then where would we move?

> 10. There are plenty of apartments in Olsberga.

11. In that case, the children will have to change schools, and they will lose all their friends.

> 12. There are probably many teachers that are better out there, and the children would not have as far to school.

13. They might get bullied.

> 14. Why would they? They have always been well liked and popular.

15. There are a lot of problems in Olsberga and my children might end up in a bad crowd and start smoking and drinking.

> 16. Why would they do that all of a sudden? That has not happened before.

17. If they do not make new friends, they might start hanging out with kids who do drugs.

> 18. And so on.

19. And so on.

Ruminations can go on for a long time. There are really no boundaries for how long they might go on. Hereby, the intelligence and imagination of human beings become a burden.

What drives ruminations and broodings?

Why is it so hard to make the hurtful thoughts disappear, even though you really want them to? What is the reason that ruminations go on and on despite our efforts to quit? What mechanism makes it persist even though we do "everything" to rid ourselves of it? Most of us have, at one point or another during our lives, wanted to end our ruminations instantly.

In order to clarify what drives ruminations I have to describe the driving force of human behavior, namely *"reinforcement"*.

Reinforcement

We know from behavioral psychology and behavioral analysis that volitionally/voluntary, controllable behaviors are driven by their reinforcers. Reinforcement is something that is experienced as a positive or pleasant consequence of a behavior, which in turns increases the frequency of the behavior. Reinforcement always follows the behavior which is reinforced and influences the use of that behavior in the future.

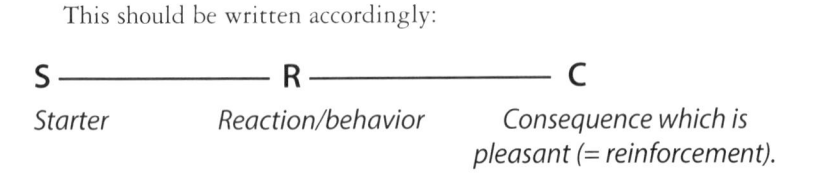

This should be written accordingly:

S ——————— R ——————— C
Starter   *Reaction/behavior*   *Consequence which is*
                                              pleasant (= reinforcement).

The pleasant consequence (C) makes the behavior (R) increase. The behavior will be repeated and more often so due to the fact that it led to a positive or pleasant consequence (C). If a child skips with a jump rope (R) and finds it amusing (C), the child will skip with a jump rope again. The behavior to skip with a jump rope is reinforced, and what happens is called reinforcement.

Premack's principle

A researcher named David Premack made an observation that came to be of major importance for the understanding of human behavior. He claimed that certain behaviors were self-reinforcing.

The activities that we choose to spend time on are the kind that are reinforcing in and of themselves. This means that these behaviors do not need any other reinforcement in order to be repeated or sustained. They are so pleasant and nice that they are their own reinforcements – we do certain things because they are fun.

Premack then thought that these self-reinforcing behaviors must be able to function as reinforcements for other, less pleasant behaviors, if they follow immediately after these. We recognize this as the grandma law, and we often apply it in our child rearing. We tell our children that they have to do their homework before they can play computer games. To play computer games is a self-reinforcing behavior which leads to homework being done faster while making it more fun to do, since doing homework leads to the fun computer gaming. As such, computer gaming reinforces doing homework.

A behavior that leads to a self-reinforcing behavior is reinforced, and is hence repeated and carried out more often. This is Premack's principle.

```
                    Behavior            Reinforcement
S ——————————— R ——————————— C
                 cleaning one's room   is allowed to play football
```

Pelle will clean his room more often because he knows that immediately afterwards, he will be allowed to play football. To play football reinforces the behavior to clean his room, since he enjoys playing football.

In the same way, a pleasant and comforting thought reinforces a preceding, discomforting thought. A liked behavior reinforces a less liked behavior.

```
S ——————————— R ——————————— C
              Thinks a discomforting   Thinks a comforting thought
              thought
```

If Pelle thinks painful, anxiety-provoking and discomforting thoughts (R), and immediately afterwards thinks calming/comforting thought (C), the discomforting thought (R) will be reinforced. The behavior of thinking calming comforting thoughts (C) will hence function as reinforcement for the discomforting thoughts (R), according to Premack's principle. In behavioral therapeutic theory, this is the reason that makes it hard to quit ruminating.

You want to quit the painful, anxiety-provoking and worrying thoughts, but you do not wish to quit the comforting, calming and reassuring thoughts. This is part of the explanation to why it is so hard to get rid of discomforting thoughts.

It is nice to take off shoes that are too small

I had a friend who jokingly used to say: "I always buy shoes that are too small because it is so nice to take them off." There is something in this joke. It resembles the motivation for ruminating. If you want to feel comfortable in that way, the only chance to do so is to put on shoes that are too small over and over. If you want to feel eased and comforted, the only chance is to first make sure that you have something that requires comforting. In order to experience a small part of the security that the comforting thoughts entail, you first need to feel discomfort.

The comforting thoughts reinforce the discomforting thoughts and make them return and multiply. It does not matter that the discomforting thoughts are painful and unpleasant when the reinforcement that follows just increases their number and variety.

> Ruminations are driven by the shifting between the unpleasant thoughts and the comforting thoughts. The comforting thoughts reinforce the discomforting thoughts, which in turn increase in number.

Yet another piece of the puzzle needs to be added in order for us to understand how ruminations function, and it is about how chains of behavior or thoughts work.

Ruminating is a chain of thoughts

We perform a lot of behaviors in chains. Anything from putting on a shirt to riding a bicycle, playing the piano or driving are examples of behavioral chains. All major and joint behaviors are behavioral chains where every small, well performed partial behavior leads to reinforcement which triggers the next partial behavior.

What Drives Ruminations and Broodings?

Allow me to illustrate a behavioral chain with the vacuum-cleaning example. You vacuum the left corner (R_1) and observe with pleasure how the dust bunnies disappear (C_1), this serves as an impulse (S_2) for you to move the nozzle to the carpet to vacuum there (R_2), and when you hear pebbles rattling in the tube (C_2), you are pleased and know that (S_3) it is now time to move the nozzle of the vacuum cleaner again.

$$S_1 - R_1 - C_1 = S_2 - R_2 - C_2 = S_3 - R_3 - C_3 = S_4 - R_4 - C_4 = S_5 \text{ and so on}$$

This formula illustrates how behavior analysis would transcribe such a chain. S is a starter for (R_1) which gets is reinforcement (C_1). This reinforcement also acts as the trigger (S_2) for the next partial behavior (R_2) whose reinforcement (C_2) acts as the trigger for the next behavior (R_3) and so on.

Let us now look at the behavioral chain in ruminating as a chain of behaviors. Ruminating consists of the two parts, the discomforting thoughts (R), and the comforting thoughts (C). The comforting thoughts act both as reinforcements for discomforting thoughts as well as a trigger (S) for thinking the next discomforting thought (R_2). Rumination is driven forward by the comforting thoughts.

> At the same time that the comforting thought thwarts the discomfort that the discomforting thought brings, which is pleasant, it also triggers the next discomforting thought. The result becomes a behavioral chain, driven by the effort to thwart/ reduce or eliminate discomfort.

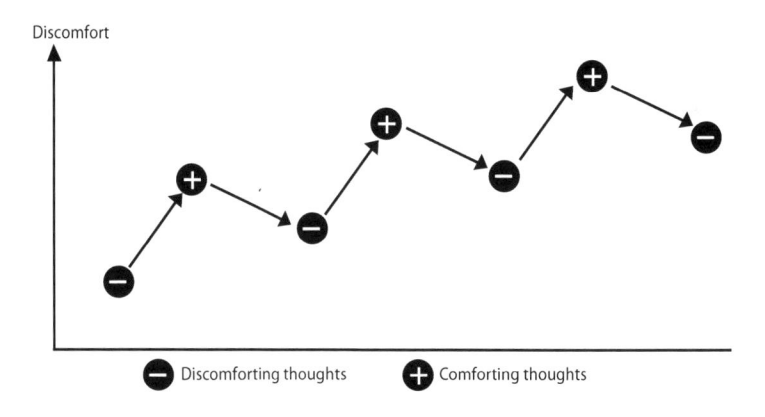

27

We now understand the dynamics of ruminating, but we still do not have an explanation as to why we feel so bad when we ruminate. The answer to this is conditioning.

Conditioning – how to make oneself afraid of one's own thoughts

If you get thrown off a horse you need to get back in the saddle as soon as possible. Everyone who has ridden a horse knows this. If you do not get back in the saddle immediately after being thrown off, you will automatically be scared of horse riding in the future.

If you perform some anxiety-lowering safety-behavior, such as avoidance or escaping, when you are frightened or feel anxiety, you get more scared of the thing you avoid or escape from. The thing that you leave or protect yourself from gets the "blame" for the anxiety, even if it was not originally the thing that frightened you.

And this will, in the future, trigger automatic fear or conditioned fear. Hence, you teach your autonomous nervous system to be automatically frightened of something that used to be neutral or harmless. It is called conditioning when a previously completely neutral stimulus has turned into a conditioned stimulus, a "trigger" for anxiety.

Little Albert, only a year old, sat playing with a white rat. While the boy sat there, someone snuck up behind him and banged two metal objects. Sudden noises are natural frighteners, and Albert was naturally very frightened. The boy started to scream and cry. The rat was instantly removed from him. They helped him to escape the rat, even though it was not the rat that had frightened him.

He calmed down after a little while and the rat was not with him at the time. After this, Albert was automatically frightened and started to scream as soon as he saw the rat. Albert was conditioned to be frightened by the rat. The rat, which had become a conditioned stimulus, which means that Albert's nervous system had learned to automatically trigger fear as soon as he saw the rat.

How did things turn out this way?
Albert had his attention directed towards the rat when he was frightened. The rat was removed and was not visible to him when he calmed down again. Fear (anxiety) and the presence of rat were connected, and calm was connected to the absence of rat.

> An object or an event may acquire frightening characteristics if it disappears from you when you are frightened and is not with you when you are calming down. What happens is called conditioning, and the thing that acquires the automatically frightening characteristic is called a conditioned stimulus.

The fact that it was other people who removed the rat from Albert, and that he himself did not escape is of no importance. Only the fact that the rat was with Albert when he had anxiety, but was not there when he was calmed made him frightened of the rat. In the same way that Albert became frightened of his favorite rat, it is possible to become frightened by natural occurrences like standing in line, riding a bus, going to the movies, or the heart skipping a beat.

When you ruminate, you escape your discomforting thoughts with the help of your comforting thoughts. This leads to feelings of increased discomfort from the discomforting thoughts. As soon as conditioning has occurred, the discomforting thoughts automatically trigger discomfort. They have become conditioned stimuli for unpleasantness.

Escape, avoidances, and other safety-behaviors increase the sensitivity for the things that you escape or insure yourself against. In attempting to disprove, avoid or distract yourself from discomforting thoughts with comforting thoughts, you make them more frightening, painful and unpleasant.

When discomforting thoughts become increasingly discomforting through conditioning, it feels even more pressing to thwart them with more comforting thoughts. This makes discomforting thoughts even more discomforting, and may result in a vicious circle.

WHAT DRIVES RUMINATIONS AND BROODINGS?

Discomfort

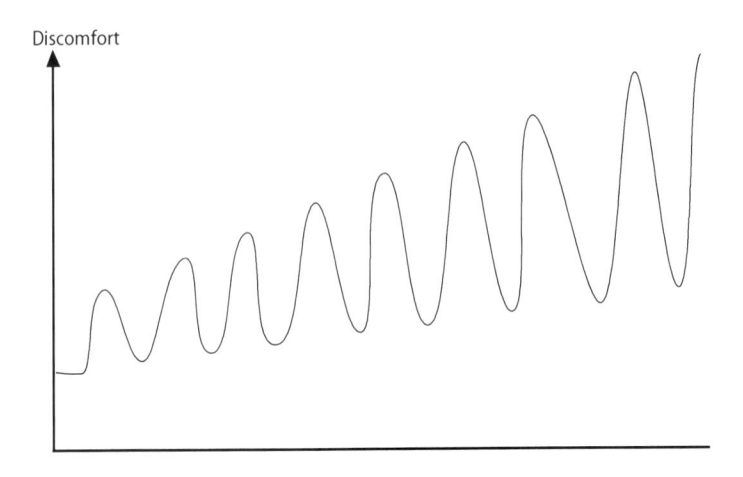

Comforting thoughts make you feel more discomfort in the face of discomforting thoughts through conditioning. This makes it feel even more necessary to use comforting thoughts to thwart the increased discomfort. In the long term, comforting thoughts make you feel worse from your discomforting thoughts, and even lead to more discomforting thoughts.

Generalization

When Albert had become conditioned to be afraid of the rat he escaped in any way possible from his white rat. With his safety-behaviors, he kept his conditioned fear alive, and another thing also happened. His fear spread to other rat-like objects. He was frightened by a white rabbit, later he was frightened by a piece of white cotton waste, and even a man with a great white beard. This is called generalization.

To apply safety-behaviors in order to escape things that scare us makes objects that are similar to what we are afraid of frightening. The fear "contaminates" things that resemble the things you were initially afraid of.

The more you try to escape from and fight your discomforting thoughts with the help of comforting thoughts, the more frightening the discomforting thoughts become, and the more often they appear. Generalization also makes new thoughts that are close to the initial thought frightening – compare the rabbit, the rat, a white piece of waste cotton and a great white beard.

The human brain also has an incredible ability to relate and connect old experiences and thoughts to ongoing thoughts. This, along with generalization, leads the contents of the discomforting thoughts to become increasingly distanced from the initial discomforting thought. The more comforting thoughts, the more imaginative the contents of the discomforting thoughts may become – even unrealistic. In the end, it is possible that you feel bad from completely illogical thoughts, even though your common sense tells you that these thoughts are not true.

The common sense in the comforting thoughts is no match for the conditioned discomfort that the discomforting thoughts automatically conjure up. You cannot fight conditioned feelings with logic and logical comforting thoughts.

> Comforting thoughts make the contents of discomforting thoughts increasingly different, more fantastic and unrealistic. This is because of generalization.

You get dumber during anxiety

When you are afflicted by severe discomfort and anxiety, a number of things happen in your body. What happens is that the body prepares itself for fight or flight through a so-called sympathetic nervous reaction. Part of this reaction is, among other things, that the blood in the body is redistributed. Blood flows to the major muscle groups in the arms and legs, to make you stronger and more prepared for fight or flight. The blood is, among other things, redistributed from the skin. What is even more important for rumination is that the blood is also redistributed from the front parts of the brain, the frontal lobe, where our logical thinking is located. Hence, during anxiety, we become dumber since it is exactly this part of the brain that receives less blood.

When we have strong feelings as a result of our ruminations and broodings, our minds get temporarily dulled. That is, when we use thinking and our consciousness the most during ruminations, our intelligence is momentarily dulled. We become so illogical that we do not even realize the obvious, that it is impossible to solve unsolvable problems just by thinking. We become so dumb that we allow ourselves to be frightened by illogical and apparently erroneous discomforting thoughts.

Summary

- Ruminations are a stream of thoughts or a so-called behavioral chain, where thoughts shift between discomforting thoughts and comforting thoughts

- The comforting thoughts are cognitive safety-behaviors that are used to thwart, disprove, create clarity and decrease the discomfort that discomforting thoughts trigger.

- The discomforting thoughts automatically become frightening as the comforting thoughts are used to escape the discomfort, unpleasantness, insecurity, and anger that the discomforting thoughts create. This happens through conditioning.

- A person who ruminates gets an increasing number of discomforting thoughts as the comforting thoughts reinforce the behavior to think discomforting thoughts, and at the same time, they function as triggering stimuli for the next discomforting thoughts.

- The discomforting thoughts can become increasingly unrealistic through the generalization that the comforting thoughts (safety-behaviors) create, and since we in our thinking connect related information to our momentary thinking.

- The dulling of our minds as a result of anxiety (the sympathetic nervous reaction) makes us uncritical and allows us to think and "approve" illogical and completely unrealistic discomforting thoughts.

CURE THE RUMINATING

If you experience unpleasantness and discomfort it is natural to act in order to get rid of the discomfort. However, it is exactly this inclination that creates ruminations. Comforting thoughts are the tool which is used to fight distressing, painful and anxiety-creating thoughts, which we now know increases the unpleasantness.

What can you do in order to stop the ruminating?

We know from the psychology of learning that the most effective way to reduce a behavior is extinction. Extinction of a behavior happens if the behavior is not reinforced. If one does not achieve ones goal with the behavior, there is no reason to continue it. Extinction occurs when all reinforcements of the behavior stop. One can certainly temporarily, as an act of will, overcome the extinction process, but it never works in the long run. Non-reinforced behaviors become extinct.

An example of extinction would be if a person shouts for someone to come, but no matter how much he shouts no one comes. He stops shouting – extinction. The behavior is not reinforced. It does not give the desired effect.

If we picture the rumination as a tennis-match the treatment would be to not return the ball back after the discomfort-side has served. Serve after serve is served, but no one on the comfort-side hits the ball back. Eventually there are no more balls left and the serves cease. The game is over.

The comfort thoughts are the reinforcement, which need to cease in order for the discomforting thoughts and thus the rumination to stop. By not thinking comfort thoughts, it is possible to extinguish the discomforting thoughts and make them stop.

> In order to cure the rumination one has to endure and even allow yourself to think about the unpleasant, but without using mitigating, explaining and reassuring comfort thoughts. Then the behavior of thinking discomforting thoughts is not reinforced and will be extinguished. The rumination ceases.

To endure/bear

One should not have to endure the fact that a discomforting thought is the truth, but that there is a possibility that it might be the truth. When you can stand this uncertainty, the discomfort that the thoughts produce without doing anything to question or fight them, then you are automatically acting correctly. Then, the extinction of discomforting thoughts is possible. To be able to endure and accept the uncertainty is thus a way to create the necessary attitudes toward one's discomforting thoughts. Someone might object, that there is an uncertainty, which is not possible to accept. That was the case with Tore.

One patient, Tore, who had newly become a father, had obsessive thoughts that he might be a pedophile. Naturally, he had no evidence to show that he was a pedophile, but it had become a discomforting thought or an intrusive thought in his obsessive compulsive disorder. Now he fought the discomforting thoughts with all possible sorts of comforting thoughts. He could not even allow himself to have the smallest discomfort thought, as it evoked anxiety. The thought in itself became a conditioned stimulus for anxiety.

Before he met me he had never dared to confess this thought to any other person and absolutely not for his wife. His only way to fight the discomforting thought was by finding counterevidence and by looking for signs, of it not being true. In his ruminations he reasoned with himself for and against and tried to find evidence for not being a pedophile and for not being able to be one.

The ruminations had now troubled him for months. I was the first person to which he confessed the repulsive discomfort thought to. The theme was not a new one to me. It is not uncommon that new parents get such thoughts, which makes them afraid that they will harm their own children. Fear of strangling or stabbing a child can also appear.

I eventually got into the theme of acceptance and enduring the idea of being a pedophile during my conversation with Tore. Upset he turned against this and burst out: "You cannot just accept this! It is not possible to accept that I could be a pedophile!" I pointed out that even if you think of something, it does not mean it is true, but you have to accept that it could be true. You have to be able to think the thought.

I explained to Tore how ruminating worked and what was needed in order to make it stop.

Exposure with Response Prevention

Behavior therapeutic treatment of discomfort states is about exposing oneself to, that is confronting that which is frightening, without in any way protecting oneself from it. The method is called exposure with response prevention. This is the foundation of all behavior therapeutic anxiety treatment. You can never get used to something if you protect yourself against it. If you are using security behaviors, including comforting thoughts, you will stay afraid. Habituation, as it is called, can only occur if you allow yourself to be afraid and not use any security or protective behaviors.

A small simile about habituation: The people who live in Skärblacka (a small town in Östergötland, Sweden, with a very malodorous paper mill) do not smell the paper mill. Visitors to the town smell it, and many feel that it stinks. The people of Skärblacka do not smell the odor since they have been blunted to it. Their noses have become accustomed to the smell, or, as one could also put it, their olfactory organs have been habituated or grown used to the smell. This is possible since they never fought the smell or tried to protect themselves from it. If they had always protected themselves from it, and worn clothes pins over their noses, for example, they would have never gotten used to the smell.

The same thing goes for getting used to things that frighten and lead to anxiety. In the long term, the method aims towards making people less bothered by conditioned anxiety and also experience less of it. It means that you expose yourself so much to the thing that evokes anxiety, that the nervous system no longer reacts with anxiety. The important thing is to not perform any safety behavior during exposure. Refraining from safety behaviors is called response prevention. You have to endure the anxiety and not fight it in any way in order to reduce the unpleasantness it evokes.

> You cannot be at peace with something that you are fighting at the same time.

Ruminating is a shifting between discomforting thoughts and comforting thoughts. The comforting thoughts are safety behaviors which calm, reassure and to some extent disprove while not being completely convincing. Exposure with response prevention in cases of rumination must therefore be carried out in a fashion where you allow yourself to think the discomforting thoughts, without mitigating what you feel with the use of comforting thoughts.

I suggested that Tore should write down all the discomforting thoughts that he had during one week. He was to create a file on his computer called "My worst thought". The purpose was that he was to get accustomed to the thought by working with it and allowing himself to think it.

After a week, Tore came back full of anxiety with half a page. The page contained both discomforting thoughts and comforting thoughts. He was then assigned the task of separating, and then crossing out the thoughts that had a calming and comforting function. He needed to learn to recognize thoughts that functioned as safety behaviors or comforting thoughts. Left on the paper were the horrible and frightening thoughts, that Tore thought were so unacceptable that he did not even want to think them.

Here were thoughts like: "What if I molest my little son." and, "if Anna is not at home, then I can do it." "If I were to bathe him now, maybe I would touch…" "With thoughts like these, I must be a pedophile." "Do I get sexually aroused when I change Axel's diaper? Do I feel anything in my penis when I bathe Axel?" "I must be sick to have these thoughts", and so on. Tore had several other thoughts that he did not want to write down when they appeared. Most reluctantly, he gave them to me. Tore felt that this was disgusting, and at the same time he reassured me that he was not a pedophile, and that he had never had any such inclinations. It was a mistake of Tore to make such reassurances, because it meant that he had not accepted the possibility that it might be true. The assurances functioned as counterproof or as safety behaviors and were in fact comforting thoughts. Tore did not dare to expose himself to the discomforting thoughts that constantly kept popping up in his head. Exposure requires acceptance of a thought as a thought, while realizing the possibility that it might be true.

> To accept does not mean that you believe that the thought is accurate, however, the possibility that the thought could be accurate is not out of the question. Acceptance is to acknowledge the worst possible scenario as possible and to allow yourself to feel bad.

Tore was then given the task to read these frightening thoughts for 20 minutes each day and refrain from every counterproof (comforting thoughts). He was not allowed to look for mitigating circumstances or a lack of logic in the frightening thought, and not to try to circumnavigate it with unreserved positive thinking.

He was also made to understand that it was desired that he started to act as if he did not have any frightening thoughts, or that he at least did not pay them any mind. He should no longer strive towards having Anna home as a reassurance when he was bathing Axel. He was not going to avoid changing diapers. He was to act and think as if he never had any frightening thoughts at all. He was to act as if he was not afraid of being a pedophile, even though it was exactly this that evoked so much unpleasantness and anxiety.

Part of the homework was also that he should actively and vividly imagine that the worst thing possible might be true. Tore was to be aware of, and present in this thought, even if it was painful. The anxiety and unpleasantness that would arise from this was to be accepted as a natural and desirable result of the exercise.

Crestfallen, Tore returned after a week. The anxiety was still unbearable when he read the frightening thoughts. Even more frightening thoughts had come up. Tore had had sleepless nights of ruminations. It is very likely that he allowed himself to ruminate by thinking comforting thoughts. This was probably the reason that the unpleasantness had not decreased.

Tore went home with the same homework, but this time with a new instruction. As soon as he started ruminating, that was even when he thought comforting thoughts, he would take out his paper and read it, or sit at the computer and work with the document "My worst thought". The point of this was to get Tore to make an incompatible behavior of thinking his comforting thoughts, that was, to think of the worst thing imaginable. To work with the document "my worst thought" is incompatible with thinking comforting thoughts.

Tore was now leaving desperate voicemails on my answering machine about how his nights were now filled with anxiety. From the times at which he called me I could tell that he had been up at nights and that he was obviously tormented by a lot of anxiety.

At our next session, Tore stated that things had gotten worse than he could ever have imagined. It did not feel sane to just be able to think that it might be possible, that he could perform pedophilic acts towards his son.

It took close to six months before Tore could clearly notice that his reactions to his horrific thoughts had decreased. At the same time, he had also started doing things that he previously avoided for safety reasons. For example, he could bathe his son when his wife was not at home.

It was not until Tore really "took the risk" and started to behave as if his frightening thoughts were not dangerous, that he felt that the fear was letting go.

All safety behaviors need to go

For ruminations to be able to stop, Tore needs to refrain from all safety behaviors, not just the comforting thoughts. It is not enough to just change your thoughts, if this is not accompanied by the same changes in the external behavior. Extinction must happen on all fronts. The person must fully and completely refrain from all behaviors that calm and give reassurance, both comforting thoughts as well as visible behaviors.

After about a year, Tore reported that he was no longer afraid of his discomforting thoughts or his worst thoughts. Uninvited discomforting thoughts came more seldom and were no longer unpleasant. Tore was however dedicated and kept working with his worst thoughts, though they did not appear very often.

Learn to recognize the comforting thoughts

One reason that it took Tore such a long time to come to terms with his ruminating could be that he did not recognize his comforting thoughts and that he therefore reinforced the discomforting thoughts from time to time by thinking comforting thoughts.

It is probably easier to recognize your discomforting thoughts than to recognize your comforting thoughts. The discomforting thoughts are characterized by unpleasantness, while the ability of comforting thoughts to evoke concern is smaller.

Comforting thoughts come in many forms and shapes. The only thing that they have in common is that they function as safety behaviors – as an escape or avoidance from anxiety and insecurity, and as an escape from the discomforting thoughts.

Comforting thoughts can be:

Logical disproving thoughts, as for example reasoning concerning plausibility. It is also common that people around you, with good intentions, will help with this type of logical arguments. Even therapists can at times give their patients logical counter arguments, but then they only assist in keeping ruminations going.

Manipulations of history "what if I would have", "why didn't I…". Manipulation can be a thought-game, where alternative courses of events or scenarios pass by. Even though they never happened, and cannot be changed in hindsight, these thoughts can be momentarily anxiety-reducers.

Thoughts of revenge, are about getting satisfaction, revenge or hopes of harming others. Especially if the discomforting thoughts are about injustices, this type of comforting thoughts are common.

Wishful thinking which say that everything will be alright if only this or that thing happened. They are comforting like daydreams.

Explanatory thoughts that seek the answer to the question : Why?. The explanatory thoughts can also be those that provide assurance, notifications and provide a sense of control. "I finally know why!" They are used in order to clear out doubt and insecurity. At least you want to know why things went the way they did, why you did what you did, how you could do something stupid, and so on.

Comforting thoughts provide a little momentary comfort, no matter if they are realistic or unrealistic. Their varying content sometimes makes them difficult to recognize.

Some examples of different types of comforting thoughts

The most common form of neutralizing thoughts is the kind where you through logic and reassuring thoughts want to prove that the frightening and anxiety-provoking is unlikely or wrong.

Logical reasoning

"The probability is a thousand to one that I would suffer from…"

"Other people do that without… which means that I should also be able to…"

"More than every other man who gets prostate cancer gets well. No one in my family has died from cancer yet…"

"I have never made anyone sad before. Everyone thinks that I am a nice person, so what has happened is probably due to a misunderstanding…"

"The probability to get infected with HIV and AIDS is just X% and the probability that I would meet someone who is infected is also just X%. All in all, this adds up to just…"

"All the singles who want to find someone do find someone. So I will also find someone."

Manipulations of history

"If he would have turned up a bit later he would not have been hit by that car. 10 seconds would have been enough, and the car would have passed by…"

"How could I be so stupid and quit taking my antidepressants? If I hadn't, I wouldn't have been admitted to this institution and then…"

"If I hadn't had children, I would have been offered that job as manager."

"If I would have just handed in my paper a day earlier, they wouldn't suspect me of plagiarism…"

"If I just hadn't walked in to that dirty restroom then I would…"

"If I had called mother when I planned to…"

"If I hadn't told her that, then she wouldn't have… and then this wouldn't have happened."

"If I had only waited a month to buy the apartment, I would have saved a million."

"If I would have stayed in my relationship with Lasse…"

"I didn't have enough money at the time to invest and commit to the company. If just would have had the money, then I would have been a millionaire today."

Thoughts of revenge (thoughts of satisfaction)

"In a few year's time, it will be apparent that he can't do the job and that I would have been a better choice. They will realize that they screwed up…"

"She will turn the entire staff against herself in the way she's acting. She's like a bulldozer that stops for nothing, and eventually, the others will realize what she's really like…"

"I could send an anonymous letter to… so that everyone will find out what is really going on…"

"If I reported her for… then it would soon be apparent how things are… and then…"

"When the kids are grown up they will realize what an asshole their father has been, who has denied me access to them. Then they will turn against him…"

"When my friends are tired mothers with little children it will be my turn to go out and meet cool men, because my kids will be grown up by then."

"My wife left me last year for that "Casanova". He will soon get tired of her and get a new, younger woman. Then I won't take her back."

Wishful thinking (daydreams)

"Now that they let me go it will soon be clear that things aren't working out, and then they will have to ask me to come back and sort things out."

"When I'm finally gone, they'll miss me. You never miss what you already have."

"One of these days they will realize how much I've meant for them…"

"I will invent a way to… and then all my problems will be gone in an instant."

"I will meet a new man, who will be both kinder and nicer."

Explanations

"I was sick with 100 degrees fever when it happened and there was nothing I could have done."

"She said so herself that she couldn't move out from her sick mother's, and that was why she couldn't move in with me."

"He is attracted to silly, blonde girls, and that doesn't describe me."

"I couldn't do anything because…"

"He acted like that towards me, because at the time, he was suffering from a severe depression."

"So it turned out that our son has ADHD. Finally we got an explanation."

"I must have been tricked by my doctor into taking that medicine. They tricked me with that diagnosis. (Patient who believes in having been harmed by medicine)."

"Maybe I wasn't as considerate towards my ex-husband as I should have been."

Different types of comforting thoughts often occur in combination with each other

Irma (36) came to me because she could not quit ruminating about her failed, and now ended marriage.

After a few years of marriage she had left her husband after he turned out to be an egoistic manipulator and an unscrupulous "asshole". She had several good reasons to get out of the marriage and finally she did, after it turned out that he had deceived her in many ways. Too many times, he had been nasty in a very calculated way. They had agreed on sharing everything, as proof of their love to one another. He had used this agreement to get her to pay his back taxes of several hundred thousand Swedish kronor from before their marriage. During their entire marriage, he had been very accusing and blamed her for most things. Most of his own faults and mistakes he managed to pin on her, once he explained things in his own way. He was a manipulator when it came to twisting his explanations. If he felt bad, it was her fault. It was she who could not make him happy.

For example, she had not been able to cheer him up when his colleagues were bullying him, he said. When she wanted to go see her mother, she was egoistic and did not care about him and his needs. And when she complained that she was sad, and said that they could not communicate, he then blamed this on her inability to understand him and his problems. She lacked emphatic abilities, he claimed.

Even though his track record was five failed marriages, according to him, it had never been his fault. His many explanations and excuses proved that he was very keen on showing the rest of the world that there was nothing wrong about him. Indeed, he had done everything to save the marriage, while she was impossible to live with for various reasons.

Irma decided to move out, and after a few days she discovered that her suspicions about her husband's infidelity were true. He had aggressively refuted that he had met a new woman. Irma was 10 years younger than him. The new woman was 20 years younger than him.

This was where Irma's ruminating began. What had she done wrong? Had she not been loyal enough? Her discomforting thoughts immediately evoked rational disproof (comforting thoughts), and so, the ruminating had begun. She thought that she really had done her best (comforting thought), and that she had been loyal to him (comforting thought). There were several times that she had been understanding and stayed at home when he claimed to be bullied by his colleagues, instead of going to see her mother (comforting thought).

More and more discomforting thoughts appeared. What is he doing with that new woman now?

Is she in my bed now? What could I have done to save the marriage? Reproaches, which he had formulated for her during their marriage, and painful thoughts of her own came rapidly and kept her up at night and tormented her, especially when she was alone. Every new thought that evoked sorrow, worry and anxiety was met with a comforting thought of some kind.

He really is an asshole (explaining comforting thought). She had heard this thought from a number of people by now, including her mother and her friends. Irma was helped with her comforting thoughts by her friends and relations, who all gladly testified that he was a pig etc. The ruminating went on: The new woman would probably discover this (wishful comforting thought), and then he would sit there with yet another ruined relationship behind him (revengeful comforting thought). Maybe she should write an anonymous letter to the new woman and tell her about him (revengeful comforting thought)?

The ruminating went on for days and weeks, and in terms of Irma's discomforting thoughts it seemed as if she had completely forgotten how much he had hurt her, and that it was in fact she who had left him because he was a complete egoist without a conscience.

Her thoughts circled around which mistakes she had possibly made (discomforting thoughts), and what she could have done to prevent what had happened (comforting thoughts with manipulations of history). The more comforting thoughts she came up with, the more discomforting thoughts appeared. She fantasized that she had not been sufficiently active and understanding when he was "feeling down". If she just would have listened more to him, then maybe they would be alright now (comforting thought with manipulation of history).

Now Irma wanted help with ending her painful ruminating. She could not sleep, and when she was alone she felt a great anxiety. The ruminating just did not end. Her discomforting thoughts kept increasing and their contents became more varied and imaginative as a result of generalizations.

We went over her ruminating and it turned out that she had failed to recognize several of her comforting thoughts. Without being aware of it, she had kept reinforcing her discomforting thoughts with her comforting thoughts. A few examples of thoughts that she had not realized were comforting thoughts: He has five failed marriages behind him, so it is just a matter of time until this relationship crashes. The same was true for thoughts that the new woman would tire of him because of the great age difference. And that he would get what was coming to him later. The new relationship will never last. A few years might pass before she discovers what a prick he is. When she is forty or sixty, she will find someone new, because who would want an egoistic old man to look after? They have no future together since she wants children and besides, they do not share any memories. I hope that someone will see through that bastard and that he will be ostracized by his friends. Many of them had hinted that it was not easy to be married to him, and they understood her. The marriage crashed because I never had the chance to show him all of those romantic places in Paris.

Her comforting thoughts were many and came in many forms. There were logical thoughts, thoughts of revenge, wishful thinking, explanations and thoughts with manipulation of history. They all gave her little comfort. The relief from anxiety that each one gave her served as stimulus for a new painful idea or discomforting thought.

Yet another explanation that her ruminating would not quit was that her other behaviors were not in line with the treatment of her ruminating. For example, she did not use the same lunchroom at the hospital where both of them worked because she was afraid of meeting him there. Avoiding unpleasant reminders is a safety behavior that keeps the conditioned anxiety alive. She also avoided going past their former home. She avoided using the culverts of the hospital, afraid that she might run into him or his new woman.

It was not until she could completely refrain from her comforting thoughts, and abstain from her safety behaviors that she could experience that her discomforting thoughts appeared more seldom.

A case with manipulation of history
Lars (49) came back to therapy and was deeply depressed. He had not been to see me for eight years. At that time he had been ruminating over his latest change of jobs. His problem was that whenever he changed jobs, he was concerned that he had made the wrong choice. The ruminating went on for years and he could never free himself of his ruminating as it shifted to his latest change of jobs. He was afflicted by depressions and was intermittently feeling very bad each time he got a new job.

Eight years earlier he had worked at one of his town's biggest industries, where he felt very uncomfortable. This was his second workplace and he now missed his last job, where he had also felt uncomfortable. Eventually, he changed jobs again and started working at the hospital, with similar work tasks as before. After only a few days, he started questioning his new job, wondering if he had screwed up again. The discomforting thoughts came to him: Was his last job not better than the new one? In his ruminations, he became more and more uncertain. In his broodings, he became more and more remorseful, confused and irresolute. Now he really detested the new job, and his last workplace seemed much better. As a result of extensive ruminations he became depressed.

After yet another few years, he switched to a similar and equally qualified job in another town. He was now commuting 120 kilometers to his new workplace. History repeated itself. As was the case at his last job, he started brooding and convinced himself that his last job was better than his new one. His ruminating was about different aspects. Advantages came in the form of comforting thoughts, and disadvantages in the form of discomforting thoughts. Now he wanted help.

Lars was in despair over the fact that he could not decide which job was the best or if he had screwed up again. The pressure dropped slightly when he took up his old hobbies and got it out of his head to not make the decision again, but rather accept the facts. His comforting thoughts were mainly about manipulating history. In his thoughts, he re-did his last choice of jobs over and over, even though it was long gone and irreversible.

Five years later, he returned to his second workplace. He did not have the same work tasks but his colleagues were almost the same people as when he previously worked there. The story repeated itself. Now he became depressed and cried in despair, and a full thought-tennis was coming on. Once again he wondered if his previous job was not better than his new one. His discomforting thoughts said "what if I had not changed jobs", "Why did I change jobs?", "I shouldn't have changed jobs." Each frightening and painful thought was immediately followed by comforting and explaining thoughts in a never ending stream. His despair increased the more he ruminated. The comforting thoughts where reminders of his choices over and over again.

He should have decided to accept that he very likely had screwed up, but that things were as they were, and there was no chance of him getting his old job back. Lars did not realize that changing history in one's mind is impossible.

He could not make himself accept his decisions. Very likely he is still ruminating about his decisions and is looking for new jobs. It is possible that he has changed jobs several times since we last were in touch.

Ruminating can cease spontaneously

Ruminations can cease without a person actively doing anything. What has happened in these cases is that the person without thinking about it has quit all comforting thoughts. This usually happens when you get so tired of ruminating that you accept the situation on your own. You give up.

It is essential to not attempt to change the contents of the discomforting thoughts, but to rather accept these thoughts for what they are, regardless of how unpleasant their contents are. It is not until you give up the attempts to alter the discomforting thoughts that counter-conditioning may occur, and the discomforting thoughts lose their discomforting abilities. The sad thing in these cases is that ruminations can have been ongoing for months, and maybe even years, tormenting the person who had them. This is why it is important to not fight the contents of your discomforting thoughts.

In moments of anxiety, never try to alter the contents of the discomforting thoughts, and do not in any other way try to decrease the discomfort/worry.

How to cope with ruminations is summarized very well by the Serenity Prayer.

The Serenity Prayer

"God, give me grace to accept with serenity the things that cannot be changed"
Comment: Accept the things that have happened and those things that you really cannot change. Accept that unpleasant things can happen in the future and that you cannot affect this with your thoughts. Think on this in all its terrifying form, endure it to its full extent so that you can get used to it. Endure feeling bad, since it will lead to serenity in the long term.

"Give me courage to change the things which can be changed"
Comment: Realize that the only thing that is possible to change is your own behavior here and now. You can decide on doing the things that are hurtful and evokes anxiety, concerns and unpleasantness. You can behave freely and not allow unpleasantness and anxiety to run your life, and instead let you values and desires decide how you will behave. You can change your behavior and your comforting thoughts and make certain that anxiety will not run you. Refrain from obviating uncertainties and worries. Dare to stay in the discomforting feeling.

"Give me the wisdom to distinguish the one from the other"
Comment: If you cannot distinguish between what cannot be changed and what can be changed you will end up ruminating. You will be tempted to try to change with your mind things that cannot be changed, which is ruminating.

Is it always wrong to fight thoughts that lead to anxiety and doubt?
Should you never fight or disprove discomforting thoughts? Should you not do that when they are obviously untrue, wrong or illogical?

No, not really. If a discomforting thought has become an anxiety-trigger, a conditioned stimulus for concern, no logical arguments will work on it. You cannot counter-condition with the help of logic or knowledge. Reason cannot extinguish a conditioned thought, and it will not work with anxiety. The autonomous nervous system is illogical, something that all people with arachnophobia know about. It does not matter that they know that all the spiders in Sweden are harmless. They still automatically get anxiety from just looking at a spider. It does not help that they know or think in the right way.

To fight conditioned anxiety with logic is just as impossible as with arguments and logic try to get a person to not feel a bad smell. You cannot, with the help of thoughts, be unbothered by the bad smell. The only way to get used to it is through exposure.

Are there no instances where logical disproof and plausibility arguments against crazy and illogical thoughts should be used? Yes there are. It is the right thing to do when an erroneous or illogical thought is not a conditioned stimulus for anxiety (when it does not trigger anxiety), but is just an establishing circumstance.

Establishing circumstances (conditions/operations) – thought-contents worth changing

There are circumstances/conditions that affect the drive or motivation to ruminate. Anxiety is such a circumstance/condition. The more powerful the anxiety or the sympathetic reaction the more reinforcing the comforting thoughts will be and brooding becomes more likely and more difficult to stop. If the anxiety, that is the sympathetic reaction, were not there at all the comforting thoughts would not increase thinking discomforting thoughts. Relief by the comforting thoughts would not occur. Feelings of worry or anxiety therefore are necessary for painful brooding.

Brooding that goes on without feelings of discomfort is what we call problem solving. Problems are questions that are met with solution thoughts, explaining thoughts, clarifications, ideas, decisions or brilliant and stimulating ideas at their best. These thoughts are not rescuing you from discomfort, instead they are incentives and enjoyable. In other words these thoughts act as positive reinforcers.

> Sympathetic reaction is a necessary circumstance/condition for the comforting thoughts to reinforce the thinking of discomforting thoughts and thus drive the unpleasant ruminating. Brooding without anxiety is called problem solving, trying to understand, inventing, where the comforting thoughts correspond to solutions, explanations, brilliant and stimulating ideas at their best. These thoughts make the process enjoyable.

Except for the worry (worry is the sympathetic physical reaction or the term used to describe the combination of physical reaction and accompanying thoughts etc.) there can be other establishing circumstances that can increase the tendency to ruminate. If you for example have incorrect information that make the comforting thoughts even more comforting – more reinforcing – the information acts as an establishing condition, which preferably should be removed or altered.

A person has the erroneous notion that AIDS is an airborne contagion. This notion or thought leads to the air in some cases being what causes conditioned anx-iety. It is not the notion of an airborne contagion that causes the person's anxiety, but the erroneous information leads to the fact that air in some instances causes anxiety. The thought that AIDS is contagious through the air is an establishing condition, which makes it pressing and reinforcing to seek protection from air in some situations.

Erroneous information, misconceptions which on their own do not lead to unpleasantness, should be corrected.

One thought, one piece of misinformation or misconception, function as an establishing condition if it through reason contributes to turning something harmless into something frightening. This misinformation cannot act directly on its own, and is therefore not a discomforting thought, however, it does make it more pres-sing to protect oneself in certain situations and it should be corrected.

If a thought, on the other hand, is directly and in itself an automatically discomforting or an anxiety trigger, a conditioned stimulus, then it should not be corrected, no matter how crazy it may be. If you try to correct such thoughts, the result will immediately be ruminations.

Such a tough stance and advice may seem provocative. If you still want to do what is questionable/ill-advised from the perspective of treatment, this should be done only once. You then confirm that the discomforting thought is illogical and incorrect, and possibly explain how things really are. Thereafter, you should try to expose yourself to, and get accustomed to the crazy discomforting thought, rather than fighting it. Below are a few examples that show the difference between esta-blishing circumstances/conditions and discomforting thoughts.

1. Establishing circumstance/condition (misinformation that should be corrected)
2. Discomforting thought (conditioned stimulus that is used for exposure, and should not be corrected)

    1. AIDS is an airborne contagion.
    2. This air is definitely contagious since there are so many people here that are…

    1. Olives give you cancer.
    2. I probably have cancer since I have eaten so many olives in my life.

    1. Children who have parents with anxiety are more often afflicted by anxiety than other children.
    2. My children are victims since I have anxiety.

    1. Serious car accidents often happen on highways.
    2. There is no way that I am driving on a highway.

    1. Brown eyed men are more likely to be unfaithful than blue eyed men.
    2. My husband is probably cheating on me.

    1. Statistics show that 75 % of all marriages end up in divorce.
    2. Stina is always grumpy and angry nowadays. She probably wants a divorce even though she says that she does not.

Another example of what an establishing circumstance/condition might be is this book. This book is an attempt to establish new circumstances with the reader. It is aimed at creating conditions so that using comforting thoughts will no longer be as attractive or reinforcing. My hopes are also to establish circumstances that reinforce enduring the unpleasantness that the discomforting thoughts entail. The information in this book aims at reinforcing abstaining from comforting thoughts, even though this will initially increase concerns and discomfort.

This book is an attempt to establish a new way of looking at your ruminations and which reinforces behaving in ways that cure ruminations. The three pieces of information that are essential establishing conditions are the following;

- that comforting thoughts reinforce the behavior to think even more discomforting thoughts.
- that comforting thoughts do provide a small, temporary and immediate

relief, but at the same time they act as start-stimuli for new and more frightening discomforting thoughts.

- that comforting thoughts can transform discomforting thoughts into conditioned stimuli. Hence, comforting thoughts become more discomfort-provoking and increase the anxiety, increasingly automatically and more frequently.

> Thoughts that cause discomfort, concern and unpleasantness – discomforting thoughts, should be thought and their contents accepted. Admit that the discomforting thoughts appear the way they do, regardless of the fact that the contents are inaccurate and crazy. Thoughts such as misleading and erroneous information, and which increase the urgency to get away from anxiety and discomfort (establishing circumstances) should be corrected.

Do not think positive

Sometimes you get the advice to think positive. It is not always wise to do this. You must be able to distinguish between instances when it is good and when it is bad to do so. Based on a behavior analytical perspective, it is always the way in which a behavior functions that distinguishes if it is appropriate or inappropriate.

Positive thinking can be used in many different ways. For one, it can be used as a general way of looking at the world. You try to see the opportunities rather than seeing obstacles and problems. You interpret problems and difficulties as challenges and possibilities to evolve. From a behavior analytical perspective, this is good as it means that you expand your possibilities when it comes to choosing how to act. It creates conditions for a widened behavior repertoire and allows for acting more freely and flexible.

Another way of using positive thinking carries with it a completely different function. Sometimes, positive thinking is recommended as a way to fight anxiety in order to feel better. If positive thinking is used to counteract discomforting thoughts, then it will only turn into comforting thinking. If it also turns out to be a successful and efficient way of decreasing discomfort, it will result in ruminations. In that case, positive thinking will lead to more discomforting thoughts.

> Positive thinking must **not** be used as comforting thoughts.

A few resources and "tricks" to do the right things in treatment

It is tricky and sometimes difficult to keep track of your thoughts' functions. It is not always easy to keep track of which **thoughts to consciously think** and which thoughts you should **refrain from thinking**. And even if you can keep track of them, it can be hard to do it right. The price of doing it wrong is that it leads to ruminating and brooding.

One possible technique is to make the comforting thoughts impossible by performing an incompatible behavior.

Two behaviors are incompatible if they cannot be done at the same time. You carry out one behavior and cannot do the other behavior at the same time. For example, you cannot bite your nails while knitting socks at the same time. You cannot mow your lawn while laying in bed and you cannot be on the phone while playing the saxophone. You cannot be considerate and thoughtful if you are fighting and teasing at the same time.

Below are a few approaches which make it easier to do the right thing, as they are behaviors that are incompatible with thinking comforting thoughts.

Acceptance

Acceptance is a trick to do the right thing, and that sometimes can be enough in certain cases of rumination. You must accept the discomforting thoughts as true or possibly true. In doing so, you must also accept the concern that this causes. The word acceptance has already been mentioned several times and should therefore be explained further.

Acceptance is, according to the American psychologist Steven Hayes:

> Acceptance is the willingness to endure unpleasant psychological phenomena, such as feelings, thoughts and physical reactions, without doing anything to alter, avoid or control them.

To just accept things sounds as if you can just allow yourself to be swept away, but what is actually referred to is that acceptance is an active act. You make and express a decision to endure the unpleasantness and the discomfort that the discomforting thoughts cause, without doing anything about it. You decide that you will not use any comforting thoughts or other behaviors to decrease anxiety, concern, anger, sorrow, doubt or fear. You behave as if you were engaging discomfort and remain in it, accepting it. You do not let unpleasantness decide what you should do, and what choices you make, but rather you choose and behave based on your real desires and values.

To keep calm in the face of discomforting thoughts, and not doing anything about them can be difficult.

If you have a hard time accepting that they might be true, which is the right thing to do, you can look at their function rather than their contents.

You do not question their credibility or their contents at all, you just look at how they affect you. What consequences do they have for you?

How did you feel when the thought of cancer came up? You do not question or assess the thought, you just look at its effect on you.

You try to understand what caused the thought. Where were you, what did you see or hear?

How long and how many times have you thought in this way? You should keep track of the number on a list.

What were you doing before, when the discomforting thoughts came? Did you primarily use comforting thoughts or did you use other safety behaviors?

Did it work when you did that? If not, it is good to use another way to confront the discomforting thoughts now.

Rather than caring about what the thoughts contain and say, you look in on them from the outside. You do not confront them.

In order to do this, you should be prepared for feeling worse for a while.

> You cannot fight something while trying to make peace with the same thing. You cannot run from something while at the same time gaining bravery enough to not be scared of it. This is also true for discomforting thoughts.

Sometimes, working with acceptance is not enough. It does not have the desired effect and does not lead to getting used to the frightening things. It can be hard to understand what active acceptance is, and even harder to learn how to use it. In those cases, it is possible to make an even more aggressive onset and actively engage in making the discomforting thoughts even worse.

The technique of thinking "the worst thought"

You can speed up the counter-conditioning and the getting accustomed to the unacceptable by making the discomforting thought even worse. When the discomforting thought comes, you try to find details that make the original discomforting thought seem pale. When you have actively searched and found new, aggravating details that make the discomforting thought even worse, you write it down with all its horrible details.

You cannot think "the worst thought" at the same time as you think comforting thoughts. They are incompatible behaviors. The worst thought blocks out any comforting thoughts.

That is why it is appropriate to be resolute in thinking your worst thoughts. For example, rather than thinking: "It cannot happen!" you can choose to think the incompatible thought: "If it happens, then it happens." And rather than thinking "What if the worst thing that could happen happens", you think: "Chances are great that the worst thing possible will happen. And there is nothing I can do to stop it". Below are a few possible varieties of "worst thoughts".

The technique of "the worst thought" makes it easier to do the right thing. Instead of comforting thoughts and ruminations, it turns to exposure to discomforting thoughts which in turn are extra horrible.

The worst thought is a useful technique when it is hard to accept discomforting thoughts and when you are prone to use comforting thoughts and other safety behaviors. It is possible that you get comforting thoughts, out of old habits, before you have had the time to think of a specific worst thought. The comforting thoughts just sneak in. In these cases, it is possible to apply general worst thoughts that are immediately useful in all situations. Some examples of general anti-comforting thoughts are. "Now, I am not going to try to babble this off, maybe this is how bad things really are, or maybe even worse", or, "That is a comforting thought, and it does not convince anyone."

Many of my patients who suffer from a lot of ruminations have had to work with the worst thought. Compare Tore (above) who could not accept thinking the discomforting thought that he might be a pedophile. For many, this is a possible and useful technique. Especially young people seem to prefer this technique.

When you have wholeheartedly committed to the technique of the worst thought, the worst discomforting thought within a very short time will seem absurd and too exaggerated to be taken seriously. What actually happens is that you undergo a crash course in exposure to the frightening thing, so that it loses its frightening ability through counter-conditioning. The course is the complete opposite to when the thought gained its frightening ability, and it makes you less sensitive to the discomforting thought again.

In order for the technique to work, you must write down all the ideas and thoughts that are discomforting and frightening. Furthermore, you must not write down comforting thoughts, reassuring thoughts or anxiety reducing thoughts. As soon as something frightening appears, it should be included in the worst thought.

As a suggestion, you should for a period of time spend about 20 minutes per day thinking about your worst thought. You develop the thought and work with it continuously, as if it was an essay that you keep improving. Mainly you work with its contents, but also spelling and grammar. You should be very focused on what you do. You should be present and aware of the meaning of the thought. You should not allow yourself to be distracted by anything else in order for true exposure to happen. It is natural and correct to feel bad from the thought, and it is wrong to use comforting thoughts.

The worst thought is an anti-comforting thought that functions to make comforting thoughts impossible to think.

Original discomforting thought	*The worst thought*	*Comforting thought being blocked*
What if I get cancer?	Maybe I have cancer, but there have been no symptoms yet.	The doctor would have noticed at my last check-up.
I wonder if my report was too thin and I will fail?	My report was definitely completely worthless and my career is totally screwed.	They did not criticize it at the meeting so it must have been OK.
What if he does not love me anymore!	He is probably just staying in our relationship because he feels sorry for me, and he will leave me any day now.	He is kind sometimes, and then he probably likes me. Last Friday he even smiled at me.
So many wrinkles! I can never get any parts playing a young woman anymore.	I am finished as an actress! From now on I will only play older women, if I get any parts that is.	I will contact the director and maybe he will let me audition. The wrinkles get smaller later in the day. I will buy a special lotion.
What if I screwed up.	They probably think I am really silly and stupid. There is nothing I can do about it now anyhow.	Lisa did not laugh so she probably thinks that I am decent. Perhaps she will explain to all the others why things went so bad for me.

Beware of alternative thoughts

It is not unusual that someone suggests that you think alternative thoughts to soothe your worries. Nothing could be more wrong, if these alternative thoughts comfort and soothe. In those cases, the technique of alternative thoughts is a direct call for ruminations.

Alternative thoughts are not necessarily wrong, as long as they do not function as comforting thoughts. If they lead to immediate increased concern and discomfort, they are suitable – in the same way as the worst thought.

The only alternative thoughts that can be allowed and are recommended in this book are "the worst thoughts".

Logic and reason are meaningless
It is completely uninteresting that the discomforting thought is illogical, completely crazy or irrational. If that is the case, and you have a hard time disregarding this, then maybe you should one time, and only one time, try to state that it is illogical or crazy. But the logical reasoning and convincing must not be repeated, since it will then turn into ruminating with explanatory comforting thoughts. This has been stated previously. After this one statement, you should try to get accustomed to the discomforting thought, since logic, counterevidence, and the right information can turn into comforting thoughts. The crazy thing in this thought does not have any meaning for how the treatment will be carried out.

Regardless of how crazy the discomforting thought is, the treatment is based on getting used to it. Changing the information in the thought does not make it less anxiety-provoking in the long term. Our autonomous nervous system is completely illogical. Objective and logical information cannot remove the automatic, conditioned anxiety. Compare this to people with arachnophobia, elevator phobia, cynophobia or dental phobia. New knowledge about spiders, elevators, dogs and dental care will not decrease their dread. Logical arguments can function as comforting thoughts, and should therefore be avoided.

You should never contemplate over whether the discomforting thought is true or logical, you should just think it. You think it and get used to it at the same time. You think it without assessing it. Simply look at your discomforting thoughts as thoughts – any thoughts. I will return to this under cognitive defusion below.

Do not try to understand why
Trying to understand why things went the way they went, or why you did something stupid might give some comfort. Even erroneous and illogical explanations can give instant and momentary comfort. There seems to be a preference for a bad explanation over having no explanation at all. Even negative clarifications, such as a serious medical condition can give clarity and feel liberating.

Oh how I have been brooding over why he has been so difficult ever since he was a little child. Now I have finally found out that he has ADHD. A diagnosis such as ADHD does not really explain anything and the brooding will surely keep going. What medicines are there? why did he get ADHD?, was it something I did during the pregnancy?, what if it was about me having some wine in the third month of the pregnancy, what can we do now so that...? Despite the diagnosis, the practical problems will still be there, but the explanation/diagnosis – the comforting thought – can feel good for a moment.

Do not try to understand things that cause regret and ruminations. Learn to cope and endure not knowing.

Not everyone manages to endure the frightening thoughts and allow themselves to be tormented and finally getting used to, and getting rid of conditioned anxiety. It is very easy to let the mind escape from the things that cause worry by letting your thoughts roam freely during exposure. You might even choose to intensively think about something else. If that is the case, the aid is called "mindfulness".

Mindfulness – to be present in the moment

During the past few years, there has been much talk about the concept of mindfulness. This is a tool for carrying out exposure in a correct manner. It is no miracle cure that helps against anxiety and other psychological suffering, it is rather a way to prevent an escape from discomfort in the mind. Mindfulness is a way to behave, that prevents distraction and mental escape from frightening thoughts, feelings or situations. Mindfulness means holding on to the discomforting thought and examining it, a bit from above and letting yourself be frightened and provoked by it, so that the discomfort can be counter-conditioned.

Properly used, mindfulness holds anxiety in place, which it is also meant to do.

Mindfulness is a behavior that is incompatible with letting the mind wander and thinking comforting thoughts, which in turn enhances exposure to the discomforting thoughts.

> Mindfulness is an aid for allowing yourself to be exposed to your discomforting thoughts. By being aware, and present in your discomforting thoughts, you prevent an escape from them.

There is another way of holding on to the discomforting thoughts, and that is the so-called cognitive defusion methodology.

Cognitive defusion

A thought is just a thought. Many people behave the way they do because of a thought, as if the thought was real and its contents true. They act as if the thought itself is dangerous, just because it is about something dangerous. With the help of comforting thoughts they try to alter the contents of the discomforting thought. They want it to go away or make it kinder or more bearable. In other words – they ruminate. Cognitive defusion is a way to get a new and more balanced look at the discomforting thought, without trying to change or assess it.

"What if I am a pedophile" causes strong discomfort, and the thought is treated as if it was true. The thought is confused and mixed with reality because it causes so much discomfort that it feels true. It must be true, since things feel this way.

Fusion means mixing or blending. Reality has been fused with thoughts. And the sensations in the body (sympathetic reaction) is fused with the distressing thoughts. Defusion aims at separating or disassembling this fusion and look at your discomforting thought as a thing or an object separated from body sensations. Take it for what it really is, a thought. Do not mix it with reality more than that it is a part of reality.

Most things in reality are meaningless. Clouds come and go, there is some rain, there are a lot of people on the bus, the train is running late, people are talking all around me in the store. I might make a mental note of these things, but they do not affect my behavior.

Some events affect my behavior. I might get annoyed with the crowded bus, but I cope with it. I might get angry that the train is running late, but I will not change my behavior because of it. I keep track of what I can affect and what I cannot affect. Discomforting thoughts are also annoying events and can be seen in the same way, as one would look at a rainstorm or a crowded bus.

"Now here is this or that thought. It is a boring thought but this is what it looks like." Rather than affecting it or its contents, you just acknowledge that it is there. You bring out the thought, and observe its contents soberly and objectively. You do not back down from it, rather you acknowledge it and observe it, even though it does not make you happy.

You look at the thought as you would look at a bird that comes flying. What does it look like? What are its characteristics? Have I seen it before? Have I ever seen a similar bird? Was this bird any different from the last bird I saw? I accept it as it is and the way it acts. I do not care if it is mean or false. I can be content with it just being...

This way of looking at your thoughts – mindfulness – leads to exposing yourself to the thought without protecting yourself from it. The technique is in itself an incompatible behavior, that prevents comforting thoughts.

Look at your frightening thoughts as if they were objects that interest you. Thoughts are things or events, which can be exciting to observe, but never assess.

Defusion can also go wrong. Katrin came to me after making efforts of looking at her thoughts as thoughts, things or events, defused from her. She complained: How can you know that the thought is just a thought? It could be a sign of something real.

Katrin could not just observe a thought as a thought. She assessed it and instantly ended up ruminating. Is it true, and does it represent something real?

Defusion cannot be a way to disqualify discomforting thoughts. "It is just a thought, so it is not that dangerous." In that case, everything will be all wrong and the approach will be comforting thoughts.

Some places make ruminations worse

When you suffer from ruminations there might be certain situations or places that make ruminations worse. To be alone can be one of those situations. It is common to brood a lot when you are alone in your bed, before you go to sleep. The bed can be a stimulus for ruminations.

If you are aware of this, you can be prepared for the frightening thoughts that come when you go to bed, and be more cautious against comforting thoughts. You should not avoid your bed, but rather change your behavior in the situation and not give in to comforting thoughts while there. In recognizing your habit of ruminating in that situation, you can actively try to change your behavior. It is about changing the bed's – perhaps long drawn ability to trigger discomforting thoughts.

If you are aware that certain situations and places are high-risk in terms of ruminating, it is easier to change your habits there.

Ruminating usually happens in situations when our attention is not busy with something else or when we are not adequately stimulated. Ordinary situations for ruminations are bedtime, loneliness, Sundays, silence, boredom, nothing to do at work, when you feel down from another reason, when you feel abandoned, darkness, fatigue or hunger.

When there is a lot of activity, when you are among people you like, when you have some interesting task ahead of you, when you have to make an effort to not make mistakes or when your brain is needed for other tasks, ruminations seldom start. This can be so powerful that it can be enticing to use it as a safety behavior. However, it counteracts the treatment and should be avoided. If you occupy yourself intensely and energetically call friends, play computer games, in order to keep the discomforting thoughts at bay, then you are doing it wrong. Disharmony between behavior and the treatment of ruminations will arise.

Harmful behavior or behavior in disharmony with the treatment of ruminations

In behavior therapy treatments of unpleasantness and anxiety, everything you do to counter-condition the anxiety must be in line with and harmonize with each other. All efforts must be heading the same way. You cannot get over cynophobia by sitting around thinking that dogs are harmless and at the same time refuse to meet dogs. This is perhaps the most common and serious mistake that sabotages the treatment of ruminations. Your motor behavior is not in line with your efforts to change your cognitive behavior – your thinking.

You can never be convinced that a thought is unnecessary or crazy as long as you behave as if it was necessary, rational and wise. You cannot feel that something that frightens is harmless as long as you behave as if it was harmful. There must be a correspondence between how you think and how you behave. Thought and action must be in harmony, otherwise, the treatment of the rumination will be sabotaged.

Lotten has been ruminating and brooding over how other people perceive her. She thinks a lot about if she makes a stupid impression, if people can see that she is blushing. She fantasizes about what they really think about her. Her ruminations are about how to behave, and how things went the last time she talked to her friends? She decides to quit ruminating. The worst thought technique is used, and she decides that they definitely see that she is blushing and certainly think that she is a bit stupid. These thoughts cause a lot of anxiety.

The next time Lotten meets her friends she lays low, she does not speak very much, answers briefly when spoken to, in order to not reveal herself, she is happy that she is tanned so that her blushing does not show.

Lotten has an external behavior that is not in line with the treatment of her ruminations. She is still behaving as if it would be devastating to blush or appear to be stupid. This leads to the fact that she cannot get rid of her ruminations.

In order to end her ruminations, she must also behave among other people as if the frightening and discomforting thoughts have no validity, but are nothing but thoughts.

> The external behavior must be in line with and harmonize with the efforts to refrain from comforting thoughts. Comfort, reassurances or safety cannot be looked for in the mind or in real life with assistance of external behavior.

A particularly puzzling case

Jonte (39) suffered from hypochondria-related ruminations. He thought a lot about various diseases that he might have or that he might be afflicted by in the future.

He claimed that he was constantly ruminating. If he was at a meeting or in an important negotiation, his ruminations and broodings were constantly in the background. Discomforting thoughts about becoming mentally ill, and getting cancer were often there. Jonte also had a safety-behavior that was closely tied to his ruminations, and that was to "scan" (to feel and consciously scan his body) for signs or signals that might indicate disease. His consciousness was constantly scanning, if he felt something special in is head, chest, stomach or his legs. If he felt anything in his body, it rapidly turned into discomforting thoughts, which were then ruminated with various disproving and logical comforting thoughts.

Jonte was also performing other safety behaviors. He had a hard time refraining from reassurances. He called his therapist to make it clear to himself that it was just his imagination. It is unknown if Jonte also contacted physicians in order to get rid of his uncertainties.

Jonte was an unusually ambitious patient who willingly tried everything that I suggested. When it came to exposure, it became obvious that his scanning needed to cease, since it was a safety-behavior in the same way as his comforting thoughts. He also tried to actively think discomforting thoughts, and to not think comforting and calming thoughts after doing so. The result was doubtful.

As soon as I described the technique of the worst thought, Jonte was on board. "I want to really expose myself, so that I get massive anxiety in order to finally get rid of it", he explained.

With his usual eagerness, he started to expose himself to his worst thoughts. Jonte was a man of actions, and he wanted everything to be done as quickly and efficiently as possible. Since he understood the importance of mindfulness and acceptance of all the unpleasantness, he also applied these tools.

Thoughts like "I am going psychotic", "I am sure that I have cancer", and "I am going to die soon since have such a long gone…" were parts of his worst thoughts.

Disappointed, he called after a few days. "At first, I had a lot of anxiety, but shortly thereafter, my exposures could not achieve this", he disappointedly explained. Now, when he thought his worst thought, he was instantly calmed. What had happened?

After a new behavior analysis it became clear that Jonte was so efficient in his exposures that his nervous system had very quickly been counter conditioned or accustomed to the worst thoughts. His nervous system had instead learned (through conditioning) that the worst thoughts became stimuli for calm. The strange thing had happened – the thoughts that used to frighten him had become comforting thoughts. They had now gotten an anxiety-decreasing function. He controlled his anxiety with his worst thoughts! As soon as he got anxiety from a new discomforting thought, he immediately made a worst thought out of it and was instantly calmed. The certainty that he was ill made him calm, while doubt and insecurity frightened him. The self-invented worst thought seemed harmless. This fact gave him the feeling that the worst thought was harmless, thus comforting. Could he not be satisfied with this?

Since comforting thoughts in the long term keep the anxiety going, and prolongs the rumination, we could not be pleased with this result. We now had to change strategies. The new strategy was, rather than the worst thought, to keep the insecurity he felt going. This time, our technique was fatalism.

Fatalism

Fatalism is a special approach to life and the world. It means that you believe that what happens in no way can be affected, but that it is predestined. There is nothing you can do to affect your destiny or events in your life. We are all in the hands of something or someone who completely decides how our lives will be. When and how we will die is already decided, and we have no chances of doing anything about this, but we do not know about it. Everything is hidden from us and there is nothing we can do about that, or in any way control it.

To think in the same way as a fatalist was the method we chose for Jonte.

How then, should I think when I think like a fatalist? Example:

If I am supposed to die today, there is nothing that can save me.
If I am not supposed to die today, there is nothing that will harm me.

As a fatalist, what you do is meaningless. Safety behaviors and comforting thoughts do no good, so why use them at all?

As homework, Jonte was to look at his discomforting thoughts from a fatalist perspective. If I am supposed to die from cancer, there is nothing I can do about it. If I do not have that disease, I might get something else, and there is nothing I can do about that either. My concerns about different diseases can very well be true, and I can only get used to it. There is nothing that I or the doctors can do about it. If I am supposed to die then…

Now, Jonte reported that his anxiety was kept alive for a longer period. We were very pleased with this. The fatalist uncontrollability remained frightening. Looking at his discomforting thoughts as fatalist possibilities did not turn into comforting safety-thoughts. This approach could not turn into comforting thoughts which would counteract with the exposure to the frightening things. The fatalist thoughts could therefore not reinforce the discomforting thoughts in the way that the worst thoughts had.

After a while, Jonte noticed that his ruminations at times ceased during the day. The extinction of the discomforting thoughts had begun, since they no longer were reinforced by comforting behaviors, and the gaps in his ruminations became bigger and bigger. Surprised and amazed, Jonte stated that his anxiety had decreased significantly and that he was feeling well.

Jonte's story shows that you must be very adaptable and continuously update your behavior analysis, since the functions of a behavior can change during treatment. In Jonte's case, the thing that had previously been a conditioned stimulus and a discomforting thought turned into a comforting thought and a safety-behavior. If this had not been noticed, the treatment of his ruminations would have failed.

Nothing is clear and one-sided, so fatalist thoughts can also function as comforting thoughts. Thoughts of being a pedophile can seem less discomforting and less frightening if it was predestined that someone is a pedophile. You must be watchful of your thoughts and other behaviors' functions in order to know how to handle them. One thought can be a comforting thought for one person, while that same thought may be a discomforting thought for someone else.

What happens to ruminations during behavior therapy?

As in any exposure treatment, where you expose yourself to your conditioned stimuli (your automatic triggers), without performing a safety behavior, the anxiety will initially get worse. You temporarily feel worse. This is natural, since the safety-behaviors/comforting thoughts, that lessen the discomfort are no longer used. The development of the ruminations, if you keep refraining from safety behaviors, is presented in the graph below.

What happens to ruminations during behavior therapy?

Figure legend:
- - - - Discomforting thoughts
——— Anxiety, sympethetic reaction
+ + + + Comforting thoughts, safety behavior

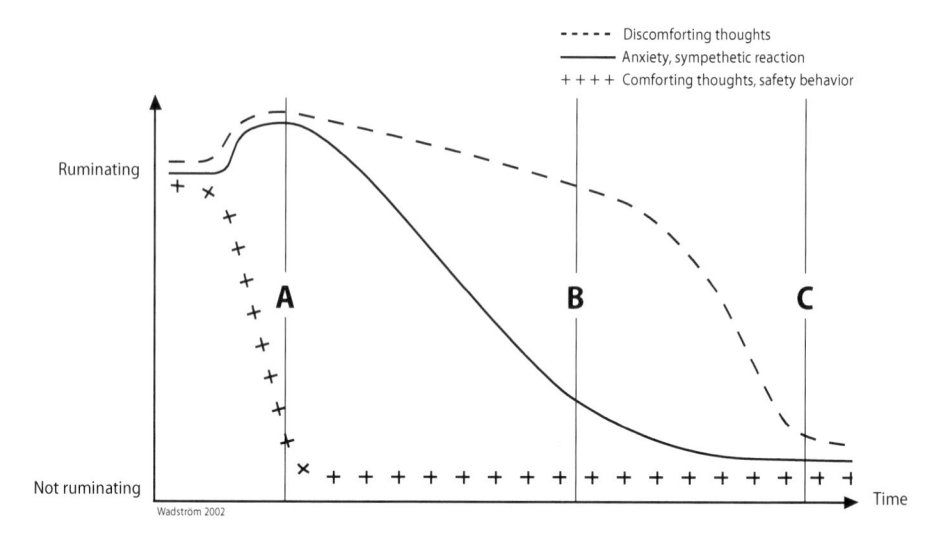

Points labeled A, B, C along the time axis. Y-axis ranges from "Not ruminating" to "Ruminating".

Wadström 2002

The treatment process is an extinction process where the discomforting thoughts are extinguished. Extinction happens if the behavior is no longer reinforced by any comforting thoughts or other safety behaviors. The graph shows that when the comforting thoughts are brought down to the levels of a non-ruminator (see point A), both anxiety and discomforting thoughts at first increase. You feel noticeably worse. The frightening and tormenting thoughts will initially come more often, in larger numbers and stronger.

The increase of the discomfort and the unpleasantness is called the peak of extinction and is a sign that the treatment is going in the right direction. However, it is not certain that you feel worse in every instance when you refrain from your comforting thoughts.

Depending on how consistent you can be in refraining from comforting thoughts, you will reach a point where the frightening thoughts are no longer capable of provoking anxiety to the same extent (point B). This means that counter-conditioning has occurred. The anxiety that the thoughts are capable of causing is smaller and not as frequent.

The improvement can be noticed when you find interruptions in the discomforting thoughts. They come and go, and an increasing amount of time passes between the episodes.

Often in retrospect, you will state that the discomforting thoughts are disappearing. The typical situation is that you discover the improvement when you are no longer looking for it. So, at the same time as it is possible to state that you feel better, you instantly begin to feel worse again. This is completely normal. Suddenly you become aware of, and start to think about your problem again. The disappointment that this causes you will just have to accept. If you keep refraining from arguing with yourself with comforting thoughts, the improvement will continue.

The discomforting thoughts will not cease until much later. At this stage (after B), the frightening thoughts are just as many as when the treatment started, but they do not cause as much discomfort. Perhaps they do not cause any discomfort at all. If you at this point (between B and C), when there are just discomforting thoughts and barely any anxiety left, are tempted to use comforting thoughts, the ruminations will quickly start over again. I have seen this many times in my clients. In order to decrease the risk of this happening, you can actively think incompatible thoughts (see My worst thought above).

How long will it take to reach point C? How long will it take to get rid of discomforting thoughts?

Some factors that matter for the success of the treatment and how long it will take

For how long have the ruminations been going on? For how long has the person had ruminating thought-chains? It is with learning of thought-behaviors as with other behaviors that they are more attached if they have been practiced for a long time. If you have a long history of ruminating, then it will be harder to consistently carry out the treatment in the right manner.

Essential for success is that you manage to separate your frightening thoughts and your comforting thoughts, and thereafter consistently refrain from thinking comforting thoughts. Are you prepared to accept that you will feel bad in the beginning of the treatment? Another decisive factor is how dedicated you are in blocking comforting thoughts by thinking your worst thought or in accepting way remain in the unpleasantness through mindfulness.

One obstructing circumstance is if there are people around, who out of kindness stimulate a continuation of the ruminating through comforting comments and reassurances. To get reassurances is ruminating with the help of someone else. If you have family members, who out of kindness, or a therapist, who out of ignorance, assists in comforting and reassuring, it is necessary to handle your treatment of you ruminations on your own.

You also have to take responsibility to care for that the external behavior is in line with not thinking comforting thoughts. There must be harmony between thoughts and external behavior. Nobody can go through the treatment in somebody else's place. You have the full responsibility for going through the treatment on your own. You can cheat and trick everyone, including yourself, but you can never trick your nervous system. You will never be free of all your problems until you do what is really necessary. If you are impatient and expect quick results, you have an approach that is bound to make things go wrong. Ruminating is exactly that, a failed quick fix. Improvements will often come as a surprise, when you least expect it, after doing things right for a while.

Stop the ruminating right from the start

It is always better to prevent damage than to repair. It is easier to stop a train that is not moving. It is easier to stop ruminations before they start. With the knowledge and increased awareness of the different functions of your thoughts it is easier to do things right from the start of possible ruminations.

1. When a new thought that causes discomfort or fear turns up, you must decide if the thought is about something that can be fixed or not.

2. If it can be practically fixed, this should be done if it is desired or necessary. Hence, there is nothing to ruminate on.

(In cases of OCD, the risk is that the doubt and ruminations can be about these two points. Advice: If the thought is about doubt over whether a thing can be fixed or not – decide that it is a discomforting thought. If there is the slightest doubt on point 1, go directly to point 3.

3. Decide to accept the possibility that the unpleasant, the discomfort thought that is, could be true. Refrain from all comforting thoughts and other safety behaviors.

If you follow these three pieces of advice, there will be no conditioning, and then there will not be any acceleration of anxiety.

> The absolutely most efficient antidote for ruminations is to do things right from the beginning. As soon as a discomforting thought appears, *think that it can be completely true and do not look for counterevidence, solace or comfort. Accept the discomfort if it comes!*

A summary of techniques or tools for counteracting comforting thoughts

The method that is prescribed for ruminations is exposure with response prevention. Here is a compilation of techniques for performing it on thought-behaviors.

A few different approaches in order to succeed in the art of refraining from comforting thoughts follow below. The different approaches have many similarities, which is natural as they all have the same purpose. This purpose is to enable intimate contact with your discomforting thoughts and their contents without assessing – true or false – or fighting them.

Approach the discomforting thoughts by:

1. ***Accept*** that things feel uncomfortable and that perhaps you feel temporarily worse when you refrain from comforting thoughts and all other safety behaviors. Self-talk that can be useful for the accepting approach can be: "It is OK that I feel bad and discomfort." "Sometimes you just have to cope. I do not care that I feel bad."

2. ***Take a chance*** that everything will sort itself out and refrain from comforting thoughts and all other safety behaviors. Self-talk that can be useful for this approach can be: "So what", "Never mind", "Screw it", and "Let it be."

3. ***The worst thought.*** Think the worst thought, something even worse than the discomforting thought and in doing so, you block comforting thoughts and other safety behaviors. Self-talk that can be useful in the worst thought approach can be: "It is natural and desirable that I feel worse when I think the worst thought. It is good, and will help me in a long term."

4. *Fatalism.* Refrain from comforting thoughts and safety behaviors since they have no effect as everything has already been decided by fate, according to fatalism. Self talk that can be useful in the fatalist approach can be: "I do not care about how I feel or how I think, since there is nothing I can do to affect anything."

5. *Defusion.* Look at the thought as a thought. Observe it and consider it for what it is – a thought. Approach: "There is a thought, and there is another one." True or false is of no interest.

6. *Mindfulness.* Refrain from comforting thoughts and other safety behaviors by remaining in the feeling and a discomforting thought – here and now – experience and expose yourself to the situation with all your senses. Self-talk that can be useful in the mindfulness approach: "Stay in the feeling and discomforting thought – feel and experience it. Do nothing about it, just live along. Consciously experience the discomforting."

WHAT HAPPENS TO RUMINATIONS DURING BEHAVIOR THERAPY?

– If I am supposed to die today, there is nothing I can do about it…

WHEN RUMINATIONS WILL NOT QUIT

The external behavior must be in line with your way of thinking – harmony

One of the most common faults in treatment of ruminations, according to my experience is that people do not change their external, observable behavior so that it corresponds with their new way of thinking.

You drop the comforting thoughts, you think the worst thought, but you do not behave as if you accept the discomfort in an external action. You keep protecting yourself through behaving as if the discomforting thoughts were still actual threats. If you keep counteracting discomforting thoughts through external behavior, you will keep your discomfort.

If you in your mind accept that the marriage is over and that it is beyond repair, but still avoid walking down certain streets in order to not run into your ex husband or his new woman, then there is disharmony between thoughts and actions, and the discomforting thoughts will not be extinguished. The same thing happens if you in your mind accept that you made a poor deal when you bought a house, but still refuse to read the real estate advertisements, in order to not be reminded of this. Once again, there is disharmony between thought and action, which sustains the problems.

Behavior therapy is about all types of behavior.

The treatment of ruminations must be carried out so that external behaviors and thoughts are in harmony with each other. You refrain from comforting thoughts, and then you cannot behave in a way that function comfortingly, convincingly or as a protection against discomfort.

Others can do wrong things

The therapists and relatives that out of kindness help out with comforting statements and try to fight and disprove the brooder's discomforting thoughts are increasing the ruminations. They teach the brooder to ruminate by logical reasoning, clearing away doubt and questioning the contents of the discomforting thinking. In their kindness, they provide the tormented person with even more comforting thoughts and reassurances.

Attempts to think alternative thoughts is a common cause of making anxiety worse in the long term. It does not matter if the alternative thoughts are so-called positive thoughts or if they are logical thoughts. What matters is, if they function as comforting thoughts and are used to decrease concerns and insecurities momentarily. In that case they are outright harmful.

There is no way to quickly get rid of discomfort or discomforting thoughts without making things worse. The quick fixes make the discomfort worse in the long term and support continuing broodings. All efforts to momentarily ease the pain will only prolong the suffering.

It is very tempting and reinforcing to accept comforting words from others when you are tormented by ruminations. It is also very reinforcing for ignorant therapists and relatives to assist with logical arguments, alternative thoughts and other comforting reassurances. I have, during my time as a therapist, met several people who have seen therapists who they have felt have been nice, but that they have only felt worse there because of this. In effect, they have been trained in ruminating. Gratefully, they have accepted this help.

> Learn to recognize your own comforting thoughts and the comfort that others give you out of kindness, or out of ignorance, so that you can refrain from them and not get attached to them.

RUMINATIONS IN CASES OF OCD, JEALOUSY, HYPO-CHONDRIA, AND SOCIAL PHOBIA

Ruminating in OCD

In OCD, ruminating is one of four types of compulsive behaviors. The others are actions (external behaviors), avoidances and to get and seek reassurances. What they have in common is that they all obviate doubts and worries.

Ruminations are often considered the compulsive behavior that is most difficult to treat. It is the one that is the easiest to start, it does not show and can be done whenever, wherever, and there is no place where there is a guarantee that it can be avoided. There are patients with OCD who spend all their waking time ruminating. Whatever they do, there are more or less ongoing ruminations.

Ruminations in cases of OCD do not vary in terms of function from normal ruminations, even if they can be more painful and long drawn. The treatment is therefore the same as with ordinary ruminations.

In order to not get stuck in ruminations you should strive to not do anything about it when the first discomforting thought appears. You must also refrain from other compulsive behaviors such as actions, avoidances and reassurances.

During treatment of OCD, it is even more necessary that there is harmony between external behaviors and thought-behaviors. You will sabotage the treatment if you instead of thinking comforting thoughts, do something else that has a calming or comforting function.

Below are a few examples of a suitable thought/attitude that can extinguish rumination before it has even started.

Frightening discomforting thought	The right attitude: Non-comforting thought
What if I hit someone with the car driving home from work?	If it happened it will turn up eventually. If it happened, it happened.
What if I have AIDS?	If that is the case this time, there is nothing I can do. The future will show, but I will do nothing about it now.
What if I get a knife and kill all my children?	If I would go crazy there is no one who can stop me. We will see what happens. In any case, I cannot ignore the risk and will not act as if I were a potential murderer. I will have to take the chance that I will not do it and take things as they come.
What if I am a pedophile?	The future will show if I am a pedophile. There is nothing I can solve by thinking about it now anyways. If I am a pedophile, then so be it.
If I do not think about grandma when I cross the doorstep she will die.	Grandma will die no matter what I do. I am not God, and I cannot control life and death. So why bother. Whatever happens will happen.
The passenger was picked up by an ambulance after we landed. Did my negligence cause his death? (The thoughts of a flight attendant)	If he died, he died. No one can do anything about that now. Maybe I did the wrong thing. If he died, he was probably supposed to die.
What if I gave him the wrong directions? Maybe he misunderstood me and will get lost?	If he gets lost, he gets lost. There is nothing I can do about it. It is not the end of the world. I will take a chance and say that he will live.

I wonder if she resented me for saying that?	I cannot take responsibility for how other people feel. If she misunderstood me, then so be it. You have to count on getting misunderstood from time to time.
What if I am homosexual?	If I am, it will show. Nothing is certain. There is no reason to care about that since there is nothing I can change about it.
What if I do not know what is normal behavior with children? How did I act towards children before I thought that I was a pedophile?	I will behave towards children the way others do when the time comes. You cannot plan what you will do in situations before they happen.
What if I am doing the treatment of my OCD wrong and will never get well?	I will do things wrong many times. We will see if I get well. What is done is done. There is nothing I can do to undo it.

Ruminations are a dominant part in hypochondria and obsessive jealousy, but of course, in combination with other controlling behaviors. There must be harmony between external behavior and the treatment of ruminations.

Below are a few examples of how to handle frightening hypochondriac thoughts and jealousy-thoughts. Some of the thoughts with the right attitude seem almost like gallows humor or indefensibly provocative. This is alright. In the best case, this will decrease the seriousness and provide for a more nuanced and correct attitude.

Frightening hypochondriac thought (example)	*The right attitude: Non-comforting thought*
What if I have cancer?	Cancer cannot be diagnosed until there are very obvious symptoms. The future may hold symptoms, and until then I will do nothing.
What if I got HIV from going to that public restroom?	That will reveal itself. All the other people who went to the same restroom may also have AIDS. The future will show how things are.

Am I feeling something in my stomach? Could it be gastric cancer?	I will not do anything about it until I show clear symptoms. I will wait another six months. He who lives will see.
The doctor who examined me last week may not be an expert. Perhaps the doctor did not see that I have cancer.	If she did not discover the cancer last week then it will not be discovered this week either. The future will show how things turn out. If I get any symptoms I will notice.

In cases of jealousy, the doubt and worry is about another person's behavior. Reassuring questions and comforting thoughts easily get a lot of room apart from other safety behaviors such as spying and setting "traps" that reveal things. During treatment, harmony between all safety behaviors is necessary, so that all the efforts point in the same direction.

Attitude towards discomforting thoughts in cases of jealousy

Discomforting thought in jealousy	**The right attitude: Non-comforting thought** *(examples of different approaches)*
What if she has a lover?	If she does, she does. I cannot force her to love me. She decides who she wants to be with. No use in trying to know or caring.
When he called it was completely silent around him, which was strange. Maybe he was not at work.	He is allowed to be wherever he wants, I cannot control his feelings. If he is somewhere else, that is up to him.
He was looking at that woman that we met downtown. I wonder if he thinks that she is sexy?	He can look and think whatever he wants. I cannot control his feelings. I can only hope that he likes me more, even though I do not look like a model.
I wonder who he is texting?	It is none of my business and there is nothing I can do to stop it, so things are what they are.

What if my partner is seeing Leffe at work? Maybe they are at his place now?	To each his own. I cannot prevent anything, so why even try. I will not be able to figure out what is going on. The future will show what happens.
Does he find her prettier and more attractive than me? He is looking at her a lot.	He can think whatever he wants. It is just as well that I do not know what is going on in his head. I am not the prettiest in the world and he can look at whoever he wants.

The examples above show that the non-comforting thoughts can be very provocative to think. They might seem to be completely unthinkable and unacceptable. Thinking like this will lead to a strongly increased anxiety. The more decisive and unreserved you can accept the non-comforting thoughts and dare to think about their contents, the quicker ruminations can be stopped.

Some obsessive compulsive themes are more likely to lead to ruminations than others

One of the criteria for the diagnosis OCD is that the patient acknowledges that its problems are a part of his or her own brain. The awareness that this is something that is actually in the mind can make it feel embarrassing to talk about your thoughts and obsessions and compulsions. You do not want to seem crazy or perverted.

This may have the result that the patient does not want to discuss the problems with anyone else. In that case there is only one person left to talk to, yourself, which is ruminating. The more unacceptable and horrible your thoughts are, the more you keep silent about them.

Extreme taboo obsessive thoughts, such as being a pedophile, fearing that you will kill your own or someone else's children, causing the death, harm, or misfortune of other people, or contaminating them, makes disproving comforting thoughts the dominant compulsion. A common theme among young boys with OCD is the thought that they may be homosexual. This thought is a thought that they rarely dare to tell anyone about. The only thing left to do is then to ruminate and brood in order to rid yourself of the doubts.

Summary of advice for getting to grips with rumination in cases of OCD

- Frightening and provoking thoughts pop up in the minds of all people from time to time. That some of us get stuck in ruminations, and others do not, is to a great extent due to how we allow ourselves be run by the feeling that these thoughts cause. Our behavior when we get discomforting thoughts is therefore important.

- As soon as a frightening discomforting thought comes, decide on the fact that it might be true, even if you can logically realize that it is a fiction or an unfounded fantasy.

- Decide upon looking at the thought and holding on to it for a while and observing its contents, advantageously with a certain degree of curiosity. Is this thought completely new? Is it similar to thoughts that you have had before? What separates it from other thoughts that you have had? Accept that the thought looks the way it does.

- If anxiety and doubts increase, do not let yourself be fooled into presenting counterarguments or counterevidence for the discomforting thoughts. Do not test it. Endure feeling bad.

- Think, or quietly say to yourself, that it could be even worse. Then think a thought that is even worse than the initial discomforting thought. Endure the unpleasantness that this causes. Do not think any mitigating comforting thoughts.

- Do write down the first discomforting thought as well as your aggravating discomforting thoughts so that you can read them and get used to them. Take out this piece of paper and read it to yourself the next time discomforting thoughts come back.

- Even if there are a lot of discomforting thoughts – try to write them all down, including the varieties that are worse. Look at their similarities and

contents. Spend time with your discomforting thoughts and allow yourself
to feel bad from them.

- Have a time set aside when you can take out your discomforting thoughts
  and torment yourself. Be careful about not looking for any comforting
  thoughts, counterevidence or distract or calm in any other way. Remain in
  the thought and suffer.

- Do not think positive when you are being tormented by frightening
  thoughts and discomforting thoughts. And do absolutely not think any
  alternative thoughts other than the worst thought.

- Do not fall in to compulsive acts, avoidances or reassurances from others
  to counteract your doubts and worries. This means that you should not
  exchange your comforting thinking for any other compulsive behavior.

- Stay in the discomfort and fear and sit it out. Accept floating in uncertainty and feeling bad for a while. It is precisely this that can decrease
  doubts, concerns and anxiety in the long term. Take the anxiety that you
  get from this, as evidence of your progress. After a while, you will feel less
  discomfort.

- Do not listen to all the kind people who help you with logical reasoning
  or who make you start ruminating with guiding questions. Ask them to
  quit trying to make you momentarily happier, even if you think that it
  feels good.

Ruminations in social phobia

Social phobia, or the fear of scrutiny, getting looked at or criticized, always contains comforting thoughts about safety and protection from shame. In social phobia, the comforting thoughts are about two phenomena. They are partially a preparation for an upcoming or ongoing difficult social situation and they are partially used for evaluating such situations in hindsight.

Before every meeting that causes worry and insecurity, discomforting thoughts appear. With the help of comforting thoughts, the person tries to figure out how to manage. His brain figures out the things that might go wrong – many things can go wrong and therefore, there is a great variation in the discomforting thoughts. After them come the comforting thoughts with various suggestions for solutions. If this or that happens, then I could do this or that. The preparations that the comforting thoughts give are similar to a general's plans, trying to look into the future in order to win a battle that has not even begun yet. Similar, planning comforting thoughts can also occur all the time during an ongoing difficult situation.

After a difficult meeting with a lot of anxiety, different discomforting thoughts appear. Did they see me shaking? Could they tell that I was blushing? Did I draw a stupid graph? Now they must have seen that I am weak.

Thoughts like these can be hard to leave untreated. And since you do not want to expose yourself through reassuring questions, which would make the insecurity and the problem even more obvious, the only thing that is left to do is to figure out the answers to these unpleasant questions in your own mind. So the comfort thinking has begun…

Advice for getting to grips with ruminations in social phobia

- The basic approach should be that insecurity and fear of screwing up is an experience that most people have had at one time or another. This does not necessarily mean that you really will screw up. Count on the fact that you, just like everybody else, can screw up, and that this also happens from time to time.

- Embrace the approach, that you can never predict how a meeting will run before it has begun. There is no possibility to predict what others will say or do. This is why there is no chance of preparing for how you will act back.

- When you get thoughts and broodings (discomforting thoughts), on how the meeting will go, think: Whatever will be will be. If you get anxiety, then you have anxiety. I might tremble and blush, so what?

- When thoughts of how you might screw up come along – do not duck from the thought, instead, think it further. Think of a number of possibilities that are even worse. Create worst thoughts. Tell yourself that if things are meant to go down the drain, then so be it. Think that there is nothing that you can do to stop it. Be a fatalist.

- Expose yourself to your worst thought. Allow yourself to think these worst scenarios – your worsening discomforting thoughts. **But,** do **not** allow yourself to think of something that might save you. Do not think of how you can save yourself. Do not allow yourself to think comforting thoughts.

- Write down your worst scenarios and find your way into them at least once per day, without thinking any mitigating comforting thoughts. Read them to yourself for 10 minutes at each occasion.

- Do not do anything practical in order to prevent the worst thing from happening. Make sure that your behavior is in harmony with your thinking. Do not do anything to protect yourself from screwing up or avoiding being discovered or trying not to be seen. Engage "difficult" situations without using any safety behaviors.

- After each difficult situation with other people involved, think accordingly: what is done is done. If I screwed up, then I screwed up. There is no way to change what has already happened. I must accept what happened, because there is nothing I can do about it.

- Accept other people's scrutiny, and that they might laugh at you and talk about you. You will never know about it anyways. If they are laughing, then so be it.

- Make the best out of enduring, and accept that the social situation feels frightening. And never try to clear away your uncertainty and your concerns in the moment. Refrain from thinking assuring comforting thoughts and running away or protecting yourself in social situations when your anxiety is high.

Harmony in OCD and social phobia

The necessity of harmony between thoughts and actions is of course, decisive in the treatment of OCD and social phobia. The treatment will become completely useless if you exchange one safety behavior for another. Quitting comforting thoughts to posing reassuring questions or avoidance instead, makes the problem stay.

Compulsive behaviors, the safety behaviors of OCD, can come in many shapes and sizes. They are in the group of actions, avoidances and reassuring questions and of course comforting thoughts.

In social phobia, the patient has several layers of safety behaviors. That is why it is often difficult to discover them all, and accordingly, several safety behaviors can remain and maintain the uncertainty, fuelling ruminations.

The outer, or first, layer of safety behaviors is avoidance. You say no to a party, you have "just had coffee", you have a cold and cannot go out. Here are also comforting thoughts that prepare and calculate which avoidances and escape behaviors that might come in handy later on.

The next layer of safety behaviors is preparations that are done in order to handle the unavoidable situation. You take a whisky to calm you nerves, a Xanax so that you do not tremble, you go to a tanning salon so that it will not show that you are blushing, or wear make-up for the same reason. Here are also comforting thoughts that function as preparations for how to act in case something embarrassing should happen.

The third layer in social phobia is about how to act when you are in the difficult situation. You sit in a shaded part of the room so that your face is kept in the dark, you only take half a cup of coffee so that you will not spill it, and you only drink when no one is looking, you do not talk so as to not attract any attention. You sit where no one notices you, you answer shortly when spoken to, quickly pass the questions on, or leave the situation.

The fourth layer of safety behaviors happens afterwards and is mainly ruminations. When the difficult situation is over, you ruminate on your effort. You try to remember the order of the words and how others looked when you did this or that.

You go through it and try to sort out what happened.

External safety behaviors must be avoided while at the same time, no comforting thoughts can be thought of – both before and after the situation.

All safety behaviors must be dropped when you work with your comforting thoughts. Strive for harmony in the treatment.

RELIGIOUS BROODINGS

Broodings often occur with people in crises and traumas. You might think about what is the right or wrong thing to do.

Matters of faith can also be an entryway into broodings. If God exists, or how should you live your life. Is there life after death? The meaning of life, world famine, global warming are all subjects that can cause concerns and ruminations.

Existential questions do not have any simple answers and cannot be answered. Their many answers are part of their nature. Uncertainty is their characteristic.

This type of broodings is just another example of rumination tennis.

Therefore, religious broodings should be tackled in the same way as any other type of brooding. Especially if they have been going on for a long time, or if they are painful.

You must accept the insecurity and the question marks and learn to live with them. Not look for answers or proof.

In these cases, it is also necessary to separate the thoughts that increase insecurity, discomfort and concerns from those that provide comfort or some momentary certainty. Evidence for your faith are comfort thoughts, which can cause broodings. Evidence, certainty and truth cannot be found in this context, and should therefore not be searched for.

Sometimes, philosophic ruminations can lead to you feeling clever in moments of clarity. It feels good to have the feeling that you have found an explanation to something inexplicable, that no one before you has found. This can reinforce the philosophizing and the religious broodings even more, as an extra "spice". Philosophic and religious broodings are then not only reinforced as a result of them clearing away discomfort, but also by providing a positive feeling when they lead to enlightenment and the feeling of being clever.

DECISION-ANXIETY

Decision-anxiety is really the result of ruminating in a decision-situation. If you feel that it is hard to make a decision, which is fully understandable in certain situations, then the ruminations before the decision can be a way to temporarily avoid the actual decision-making. As long as I am considering what to do, the longer I postpone the risk of making the wrong decision. Ruminations are thereby reinforced in yet another way, besides the fact that it is a behavior-chain with reinforcing comforting thoughts, just like all other types of ruminations.

People tend to avoid changes. We prefer things that are proven safe. In terms of evolution, this approach has been successful for the survival of the individual. Choosing something new, a path untraveled could mean death for a Stone Age man.

The safest thing to do is taking the path that has been proven safe before. The road you are used to and have walked down many times before does not cause as much uncertainty and anxiety as a new and untried one. The people who do not take the new road and use the old one live longer and have the chance to have more children than the one who tries something new. These people's many children can in turn inherit the aversion to new things. Being an opponent of, and feeling uncertainty and discomfort in the face of change is therefore natural, and is present in most of us. Our brain helps us predict possible dangers ahead of each choice and new decision that means change. Discomforting thoughts follow.

The discomforting thoughts in the face of decision-making are about uncertainty and the fear of making the wrong decision. The comforting thoughts can be arguments for one or the other option. But for every argument or comforting thought, that seems to clarify the decision, there are more discomforting thoughts that increase the uncertainty and that need more clarifying comforting thoughts. The longer you think about a decision, the harder it gets, because you will always find new aspects that need to be taken into consideration. When the anxiety has grown through conditioning, you can no longer think straight – you are stupefied and confused and the decision seems harder to make.

Humans have the capacity to take only a limited number of aspects into consideration when comparing and evaluating situations. The simplest decision can, if you are very meticulous and think about it a lot, lead to an incredible number of points to compare.

Let us take an obviously simple choice of a suitcase in a store. This can cause a number of factors which can all turn into discomforting thoughts. Here are a few suggestions: Size, what do I need now, and what will be most useful in the future, price, durability, material, known brand, color, appearance, wheels at the bottom, which type suits me best, will more family members than me be using it, easy to store, will the others in my family like it, is it rainproof, can I lock it, will it protect my things if it is thrown by luggage handlers at the airport etc.

Let us assume that we, with difficulty, can handle more than five important aspects at the same time during a decision. In the list above, we already have 18 aspects. The whole thing is further complicated by the first choice you will have to do – which aspects are the most important ones?

Decision situations seem to be made for ruminations since there is no "right" decision. Every possibility has its pros and cons. You can never be certain that you have made the right decision. And there is no sure answer in hindsight.

The more things you take into consideration, the harder it will be to make the decision. The longer you spend ruminating about different aspects – pros and cons – the more aspects you will find. The more aspects you feel a need to be taken into consideration, the more frightened you are of making the wrong decision.

If you keep ruminating over whether or not the right decision was made after the decision has been made, then you will be increasingly frightened of similar situations in the future. Initially, important and decisive decisions are anxiety-provoking, but after a lot of ruminating in decision-situations, even the most trivial decisions can become painful.

Here is an example of an agonizing decision over a divorce.

Decision-anxiety

Discomforting thoughts (decision to separate) **FOR**	*Comforting thoughts (get off making a difficult decision)* **AGAINST**
1. I should get divorced. My sister and my mother say so. Everyone says so.	2. No, my husband can be nice.
3. How many times has he beaten me?	4. But when he is sober, he is nice and quiet.
5. But he drinks, so I have to get a divorce.	6. Where should I live? We have such a nice house. I do not want to leave it.
7. For how long must this hell go on for a house? I cannot stand it!	8. It is best for the children if I stay. They might not be able to have their own rooms and they would lose friends and also have to change schools.
9. But they do not feel good either with a father who acts the way he does.	10. They do not seem harmed yet. And they do not want to move away from here.
11. But they can see that I am sad, and it is not good for them. I have to break this up, both for my own sake as well as for their sake.	12. Maybe I will not get custody. It will be calmer if I stay.
13. I should not be a coward. It will not be easier if I wait. I have been postponing this for a long time.	14. But the custody of the children! The Social Welfare Authorities do not know about Holger's drinking problem, so it is not certain that I will get sole custody. Lisa had to share custody with her husband, and his problems were worse than Holger's.
15. Shared custody is no disaster. A week at each place. I cannot postpone this.	16. Materially, the children would be much better off with him. What if they do not want to be with me?
17. They probably understand that it is not good or fun to live with a father who drinks.	18. Pelle does not realize it. He also depends on Holger driving him to his practice. I will not be able to afford a car.

19. A car cannot stop me from protecting the children and giving myself a bearable life?

20. Maybe I cannot protect them. They will still be staying with Holger at least every other week, without me keeping them safe.

21. And so on.

In this example, all the demands and arguments for a separation were difficult and caused discomfort, while the comforting thoughts led to comfort in their function as arguments for not having to make the difficult decision for yet another while. The more a decision is postponed, the more anxiety it will cause.

The big decision

In order to think about decisions in the right way, and not ruminate forever on the big decisions, the technique with the four squares can be used.

Get a sheet of paper, divide it into four areas like the example on the next page. After that, start filling out the squares in a sequence resembling a horseshoe. Remember to write down all aspects you can think of, such as emotional, social, financial, comfort and practical ones and so on.

Make the decision with help from this and let that decision stand. If you are in doubt in hindsight – refer to the paper and that the decision stands.

Not getting divorced	*Getting divorced*
Advantages 1	**Advantages 4**
We stay in the house	My life will be calmer
The children get to live in one place and will not have to move every other week	The children will not have to listen to our fights
The finances stay the same	I will not have to worry about what will happen
I will not have to deal with the fight that the divorce would bring	There will be no fights on the vacation or about the vacation
I will have access to a car	There will be no fights about drinking
Pelle can get a ride to his hockey practice	No fights over money
	Less worry
	We will not have to spend time with Holger's "drinking buddies'" families
	Nothing sexual with Holger
	I will not have to meet Holger every day
Disadvantages 2	**Disadvantages 3**
Continuing worry of what will happen	Financially worse
Continuing ruminations on whether to divorce or not	No car (Pelle's hockey)
Continuing worry of things getting worse	Move out of the house, live in an apartment.
Fights at night	The children will have to move every other week
Physical abuse?	The children might not be able to have their own rooms
The children are afraid and unhappy	We might lose touch with Holgers parents
Bad sleep for all of us	Less Christmas present for the children?
	Lotta cannot go to horse riding camp in the summers

Treatment of decision-anxiety

A lot of people go for the "first feeling" or the "gut feeling" and this is likely a good strategy for those who normally get stuck in decision-anxiety with ruminations.

Another possible strategy, in some cases, is to rapidly and randomly choose two or three important aspects that you decide to consider in the decision-making, and then make the decisions.

When the decision has been made, there is nothing that can be done about it. No more thought-tennis is allowed. Discomforting thoughts that say that the wrong decision was made should be met with the worst thought "Of course I have screwed up." You allow yourself no comfort thoughts afterwards. You never redo the decision process in your mind, the decision was made, and that is the way it is. Perhaps things went wrong, but it is what it is.

Since there is rarely any clear right or wrong in complicated decisions, you should never aim at making the perfect one. The decision must be accepted as something final. It cannot be altered or changed if you are to do things right from a perspective of treatment. The die is cast.

> When you have made your decision, decide that the decision you made was good enough and do not look for arguments (comforting thoughts) that it was good.

EXPECTATION ANXIETY

ANTICIPATORY ANXIETY

Not just decision-anxiety, but anticipatory or expectation anxiety is also a child of ruminations. They are very similar.

Anna was complaining about expectation anxiety. She claimed that the anxiety before and up until the meeting at the meeting at the office was even worse than the meeting itself. Anna was to do a brief presentation of the company's results at the meeting.

Anna, who claimed that she was shy and had poor self esteem, had directed her life against a plethora of avoidances that had fundamentally altered her career and life trajectory. Most of this was affected by her expectation anxiety. If she was going on a pleasure-trip with her colleagues, she lived with ruminations up until she said no, just before the trip. If she received an invitation she often said no after a period of ruminations and doubt. If she was invited to some event, she usually turned the invitations down in the last minute. Offers of new work tasks and making a career had also been turned down after periods of brooding.

Seldom or never did she get so far that she reached the situation that she was actually scared of. "Kind" parents and a "caring" boyfriend drove her and helped her with both avoidances and reassurances.

"You are really good, Anna."

"You know how well you always do."

"The last time you were just as worried, but remember how well things went. You will do just as well this time as well."

Anna got further reinforcements in her broodings with comforting thoughts. The more unhappy she was, the more reinforcement she received from her family.

A characteristic feature for Anna was that she usually initially thought that she would try to do the difficult thing, and that she after that vacillated between doing it and not doing it before deciding to not do it in the last minute.

The period up until she declined was a long period of ruminations, where the comforting thoughts where those that were about escaping, abstaining and getting away from what the discomforting thoughts were about.

"I ought to do it"

"Should I?"

"I should! I will regret it if I say no."

"It's embarrasing if I don't"

Being afraid of your thoughts

Comforting thoughts – both her own, as well as the reassurances from other people, do not save her from the real threat. They temporarily save her from the discomforting thoughts of the real threat. Through this, the discomforting thoughts become even more discomforting, through conditioning. The discomforting thoughts become conditioned stimuli and are then able to awaken her concerns and anxiety. This makes the necessity for even more comforting thoughts greater, which makes the discomforting thoughts more discomforting and so on.

For every time she escapes the discomfort in an expectation-situation, the bigger and the more discomforting thoughts she will experience the next time an expectation-situation arises.

The results of this will be that she will constantly, but only momentarily, be saving herself from the anxiety and discomforting thoughts, before the real frightening situation has actually happened.

Compare this to Albert who was rescued from the rat. Anna was rescued from her discomforting thoughts, which in themselves become conditioned stimuli (triggers) for anxiety and become even more discomforting. The discomforting thoughts turn her discomfort and anxiety so bad that she starts suffering even before she is in the situation that she fears.

EXPECTATION ANXIETY

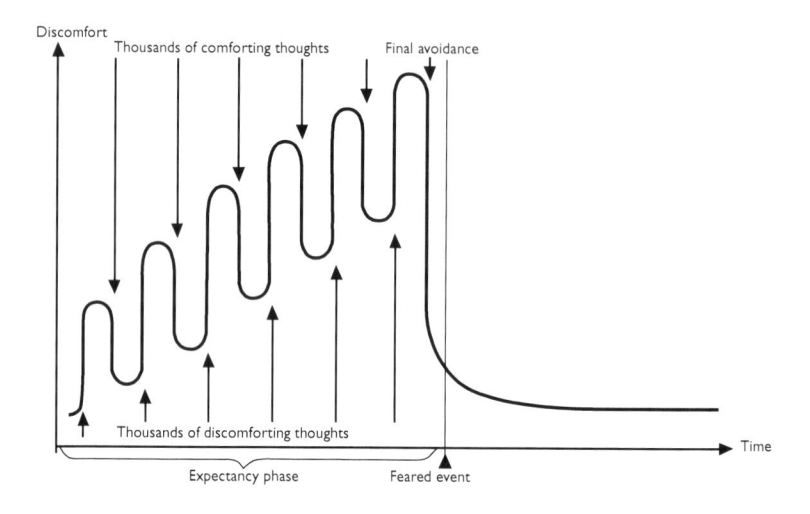

Expectation anxiety is a long rumination, where discomforting thoughts build up an even greater dread the closer to the doing of the feared you come. The comforting thoughts are about avoidances, should I say no, should I pretend to be sick in order to get off or should I get "hindrances". For every time this repeats itself, the levels of anxiety are increased.

In the image (above), the upwards pointing arrows correspond to the anxiety-increasing discomforting thoughts, while the downward facing arrows point to the temporary anxiety-decreasing effect of the comforting thoughts. The final decrease of the anxiety occurs just before the actual threat occurs. Through this final avoidance, the avoidances of the discomforting thoughts which the comforting thoughts have caused, will linger and remain unchallenged. Reality does not get the chance to prove the expectation anxiety wrong and that it has been unnecessary and uncalled for.

Expectation anxiety is to have anxiety in advance, which is caused by thoughts of something that has not happened yet.

> Expectation anxiety will arise if you, with the help of your comforting thoughts, escape from the discomforting thoughts of what will happen. It makes discomforting thoughts increasingly frightening through conditioning. Finally, you automatically feel bad just from the thought of what you are supposed to do.

How do you prevent expectation anxiety?
If you want to prevent developments of expectation anxiety, there are two options.

The first and best possibility is to without a doubt and in a natural manner do what you initially decided on doing. You do not allow yourself to quit or avoid the frightening thing, even in your thoughts. You do it without any doubts from the first point to the last, until it has really been carried out. No comforting thoughts during the expectation-phase in the form of avoiding it.

The second possibility is that you say no from the very beginning. Before you have had the time to become worried or even had the time to start thinking about the frightening things, you say no. In that case, conditioning of the thoughts of the frightening thing cannot occur. All combinations between option one and two entail a risk of ruminations and thereby, the risk of developing expectation anxiety.

Expectation anxiety is hard to treat
Expectation anxiety is hard, or perhaps even harder to treat than anxiety in the face of real things. The explanations for this are that the expectation-phase is much longer, and that the exposure to expectation-thoughts becomes much longer than the exposure to the actual thing. The treatment becomes lengthier, the suffering is longer in cases of expectation anxiety and the treatment calls for plenty of determination and will to feel bad for a long time. You must be able to feel bad during the entire expectation-phase, without starting to ruminate over the possibilities to escape.

Eva (34) had social phobia with a fear of eating and drinking with other people. She was scared of trembling and spilling things. Eva, who was a "nice" girl, had accidentally spilled a cocktail on her dress during her high school graduation, something that caused a lot of commotion. The episode had been very embarrassing. After that, she had increasingly attempted to avoid eating and drinking in the company of others. Generalization had made most meal-situations problematic. Soon, it was not just cocktail glasses that were conditioned stimuli for anxiety, but also coffee cups, mugs, glasses, knives and forks.

As soon as Eva received an invitation to a party, she started worrying. She ruminated over whether to go or not and she looked for different reasons for not going.

She avoided the discomforting thoughts, perhaps a thousand times through comforting thoughts. I will say that I might get sick, I have nothing to wear, Bengt might be away and I will not go alone. She also thought a lot about what she could do and how she would act in the frightening situation. These were also comforting thoughts. Her discomforting thoughts caused her a lot of anxiety before the party, which she often turned down at the last minute. The procedure repeated itself, and for each time, she became increasingly scared of her discomforting thoughts.

Her ruminations went on for several years and her generalizations extended further and further. When she came to me for help, even letters with hand-printed address had turned into conditioned stimuli. They could be invitations to parties. Eva's suffering extended over a long time. She suffered from expectation anxiety for weeks or months ahead of each party.

Treatment of expectation anxiety

Expectation anxiety is treated in the same way as all other ruminations, through avoiding thinking comforting thoughts. The possibility to say no should not even be considered, unless that possibility is taken instantly. No thoughts that you might get sick, be hindered in any way or some other acts of God, will cancel the party. The aim should be set on going through with the frightening thing and no hope-giving comforting thought (avoiding thought) is allowed.

It is also necessary that external behaviors harmonize and are in line with the treatment of ruminations. That is why you always do what you would rather avoid in reality.

Johan has expectation anxiety over a presentation he is to have at his workplace. He has known about it for two weeks and has been ruminating over it both day and night. In order for Johan's problems to be treated, it is necessary that he allows himself to think discomforting thoughts. He allows himself to think that things can go wrong and that he might screw up. When the discomforting thoughts come, he holds on to them, which makes him feel worse. He stays in the discomfort and is aware of it and present in it. He can even allow himself to think the worst thought, so that his comforting thoughts are blocked. He does not elaborate on thoughts of avoiding the task in his mind, instead he is dedicated to holding his presentation.

Finally, he has his presentation in a way that means that he does not make use of any safety behaviors, neither comforting thoughts, nor avoidances. Refraining from all safety behaviors for the first time during treatment is very hard, but in the long term it is essential. Harmony between external behavior and thought behavior must also exist during the treatment of expectation anxiety.

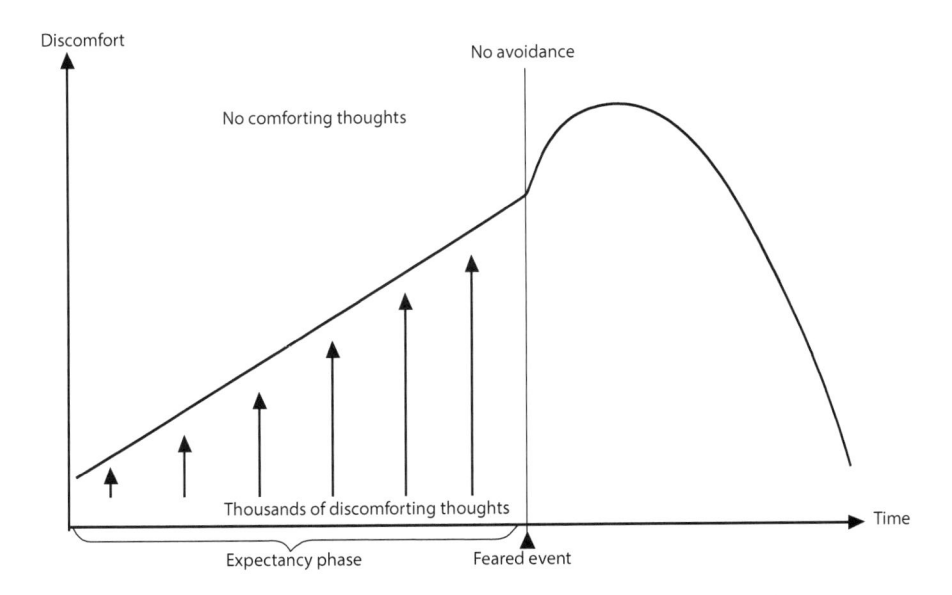

During the expectation-phase, the discomforting thoughts are accepted while the comforting thoughts are avoided. Dedication to do the thing that frightens is there from the start. Hence, all comforting thoughts become unnecessary and no longer credible, since these are about avoidances. The discomforting thoughts stand unchallenged. Carrying out the frightening thing at all costs is already decided, no matter how much the discomforting thoughts frighten.

Expectation anxiety

Discomfort

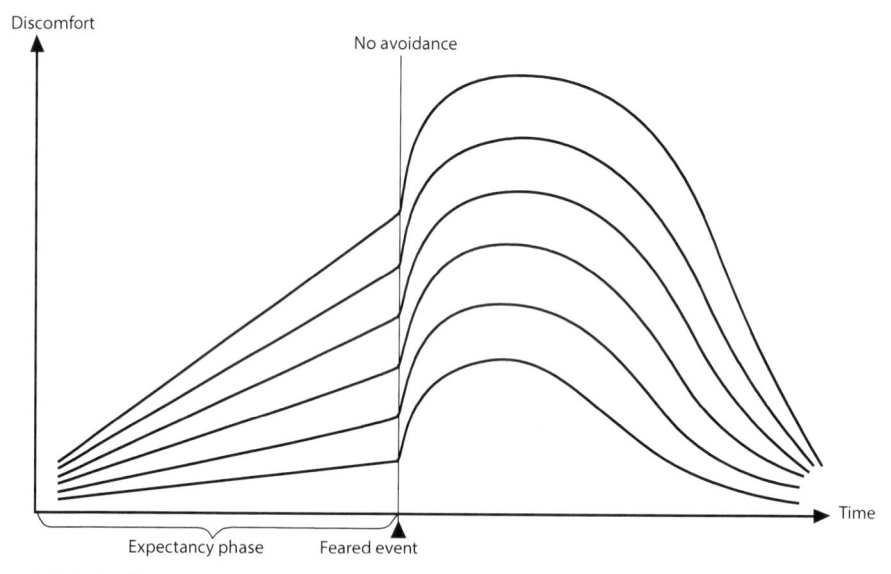

No avoidance

Expectancy phase — *Feared event* — *Time*

This is done over and over, which results in extinction of the discomforting thoughts and as counter-conditioning of both expectation anxiety and performance anxiety.

For each time you go through the treatment without comforting thoughts during the expectation-phase and without safety behaviors during the carrying out-phase, the faster the anxiety levels will decrease. The anxiety level decreases, which makes it easier to do the right thing.

The treatment is quicker, the more you practice. If too much time passes between the practice sessions, the conditioning will have time to recover and progress will not occur. Spontaneous recovery of old conditioned anxiety happens during a period of lack of exposure. That is why you should not stop after overpowering anxiety a few times. You have to expose yourself from time to time. In the beginning, the pauses should be shorter, and after a while, you might consider allowing yourself a slightly longer pause. This is done to prevent the problem from spontaneously recovering.

EXPECTATION ANXIETY

Our intelligence and imaginations often frighten us with its´ never ending flow of thoughts, ideas and whims.

CLOSING WORDS

*It was a good way to receive instant grace.
The old woman said, and ate the book of hymns*

Proverb – Pelle Holm

Buying this book is not enough for getting rid of ruminations. It is not even enough to read the book, you have to actively work with your behavior and comforting thoughts in order to reach any results. Cognitive behavioral therapy is work where dedication is rewarded.

The external behavior must be in line with the efforts to quit thinking comforting thoughts. It is also necessary that you are prepared to take the risk of doing what you ruminate about. It is fully possible to cure ruminations by acting as if the discomforting thoughts are completely meaningless, but it will probably be easier if you are aware of how to approach the comforting thoughts.

Changing the comforting thoughts must be done in line with changes of the exterior behavior. It is not enough to just change the thoughts. Either you change the exterior behavior alone, or harmony must exist between external behavior and the approach to your comforting thoughts.

Intelligence – for better and worse

All coins have two sides. The same goes for our intelligence. It allows us to plan, be prepared and protect us in situations where we are unsafe and threatened. Unfortunately, it can also make us see and experience dangers, problems and difficulties where there are none. Our intelligent minds often frighten us with its never ending flow of thoughts, ideas and whims.

Our intelligence also gives us the opportunity to try to fight things with our minds. Things that cannot be fought. This capability is the foundational precondition for our broodings.

When you ruminate, you really overestimate the power of thoughts and you act as if you can with your mind change things that cannot be changed. Ruminations can be described as our intelligence was fighting itself. It both frightens and calms us.

Ruminations and broodings are to a great extent self-inflicted. This can be affected by daring to change your behavior and thoughts. The hard part is to do the right thing, since doing the right thing feels wrong.

Doubt and uncertainty are the result of ruminations, but also their fuel. Ruminations are futile attempts at clearing away doubt. Doubt is also a natural and inescapable part of life. A lot of doubt can never be obviated, so we have to live with it.

"Without any doubts, you would not be completely sane" *quote from Tage Danielsson*.

Do not take your frightening and discomforting thoughts too seriously. Your brain keeps inventing things for you to worry about. Let the thoughts come and go as they please. Do not let yourself be run by worries and doubts by letting them make you start arguing with yourself.

The Serenity Prayer
God, give me grace to accept with serenity the things that cannot be changed
Give me courage to change the things which can be changed
Give me the wisdom to distinguish the one from the other.

Closing words

Reference for the scientific base of this book

Wadström O: When Mowrer is Not Enough: An Operant Analysis of Rumination. http://psykologinsats.se/files/files/PDF/Rumination2013_olle.pdf or just search on the internet for "When Mowrer is not enough".

Appendix A

ARE YOU A RUMINATOR AND A BROODER?

Answer the questions as honestly as you can, and think about how the past week has been. Do not fool yourself by thinking about your answer. Select the immediate and spontaneous answer. Circle your answers.

1. Are you looking for evidence or other things that can disprove unpleasant or painful thoughts or ideas?

never 0   occasionally 1   often 2   nearly all the time 3

2. Do you have a hard time making decisions in important matters? Does it take you a long time to make up your mind?

never 0   occasionally 1   often 2   nearly all the time 3

3. Do you like to tell several other people about it when you are feeling unhappy and about your problems?

never 0   occasionally 1   often 2   nearly all the time 3

4. Do you think about things that have happened or things that you have done, even though it is too late to do anything about them?

never 0   occasionally 1   often 2   nearly all the time 3

5. Do you like it when kind people (parents, friends and therapists) around you say reassuring things and help you with arguments about how things really are?

never 0   occasionally 1   often 2   nearly all the time 3

6. When you get a frightening thought or a thought that causes anxiety, do you instantly try to think positive or think alternative thoughts?

never 0   occasionally 1   often 2   nearly all the time 3

7. Do you use any tricks for distracting yourself or for cutting off unpleasant

APPENDIX A

thoughts in any way?
    never 0   occasionally 1   often 2   nearly all the time 3

8. When you feel bad – do you ever try to fend off unpleasant thoughts?
    never 0   occasionally 1   often 2   nearly all the time 3

9. Do you ask reassuring questions of other people when you are in doubt?
    never 0   occasionally 1   often 2   nearly all the time 3

10. Do you daydream and fantasize that things will be alright, even though you know that the situation is more or less hopeless?
    never 0   occasionally 1   often 2   nearly all the time 3

11. Do you ask for other people's advice, even if the decision is not that big?
    never 0   occasionally 1   often 2   nearly all the time 3

12. Do you have a hard time letting go of injustices that you have experienced?
    never 0   occasionally 1   often 2   nearly all the time 3

13. Do you have a hard time making decisions, in the store, at work, or in other places where there are options?
    never 0   occasionally 1   often 2   nearly all the time 3

Count your score.

Total score = _____

0-17 points. A low score (below 17) does not mean that you are not tormented by ruminations and broodings. It is your experience that decides if you want to work with the problem.

17-30 points. You ruminate and try to solve unsolvable problems in your thoughts to a great extent. It would likely be a good investment for feeling better in the future, if you worked with decreasing your ruminations.

More than 30. A very high score. You have a lot to gain from working with your behavior and your thoughts. Compare your score before and after you have read the book and worked with your ruminations.

Appendix B

ADVICE AND APPROACHES

for you who wish to get rid of ruminations and broodings, and have less anxiety in the long term

Effective advice that will likely be hard to follow 100%.

- Doubt and insecurity are a part of life. The only thing we know about our future is that we will one day die. Most other things are highly uncertain. There is nothing to gain from trying to figure out what might happen.

- There are no answers to many of life's questions, we must accept this.

- Be clear about the fact that it is impossible to change history through thinking. What has happened is in the past, and it cannot be undone or changed in any way.

- When you are afflicted by doubt and ponderings, quit looking for certain evidence. Simply state that there is likely nothing to be done about whatever torments you.

- Accept the unpleasantness that discomforting thoughts cause you. This is the fastest way out of discomfort, even if it takes some time to work. Impatience, in this case, is your worst enemy.

- Do not strive for complete freedom from anxiety. Feeling bad at one time or another is inescapable. Without anxiety to compare with, we would not know if or when we were happy.

- Accept the things that cannot be changed, and realize that there might not be an acceptable solution to certain problems. Look at the discomforting thoughts, without assessing whether they are true or not.

- If you are talking to others about what is tormenting you; beware of any attempts of reassurances or solutions to unsolvable problems. Reassurances cause as much anxiety in the long term as comforting thoughts.

- Chastise others if they try to convince you of things that there is no certainty in, or things that they do not know anything about. Never ask yourself reassuring questions on things that are uncertain. Intentionally remain in the uncertainty – stay in it and be aware of it.

- Do not listen to people around you who try to convince you that things will turn out alright in one way or another. Tell them to stop when you discover that what they are saying is not true.

- Avoid using positive thinking and alternative thoughts that momentarily relieve discomfort and anxiety. It is OK to think positive and to see the positive side in hardships, but not to counteract or stop anxiety. Positive thinking as comforting thoughts is just as unsuitable as other comforting thoughts.

- Stay in your frightening thoughts. The faster you do this, the faster you will get used to the inescapable, and the faster you will reach freedom from anxiety.

- Choose a therapist who does not help you with calming remarks and logical counterarguments (comforting thoughts) or who encourages you to fight your discomforting thoughts.

APPENDIX C

Appendix C
E-MAIL CORRESPONDENCE WITH A RUMINATING PATIENT

Below is an e-mail correspondence between myself and a ruminating patient, Gunnar, 23, who tries to get rid of his ruminations. Perhaps it can provide ideas for how to handle and behave with ruminations. The compilation is comprised of four months of e-mails. Gunnar's e-mails in this font.

My comments indented and in this font.

Gunnar: Things have been really tough the last few days. I do not really know why.

Olle W: Increased anxiety is part of the process, when/if you expose yourself to your discomforting thoughts, when you write them down. You are supposed to and can expect to feel worse temporarily. Now do not go looking for "are things not supposed to get better today??", because in that case, you will never feel better. Instead, allow yourself to be surprised that you feel better when that happens. Certainly, you are way too concentrated on feeling well, instead of living and letting your feelings be what they are. You cannot become normally functional and live like average people if you are constantly checking how you feel, and do nothing else than keeping track of this.

Gunnar: I have so many thoughts all the time that make me completely unfocused, which creates even more anxiety and thoughts. Last night I felt panicky (I am usually able to relax at night). I do not want to feel too much, but at the same time it is frustrating not knowing why I am feeling bad, plus, I want to be able to write down why, when and what thoughts I have, like we said I should. It feels necessary to find out, but it also creates a bigger risk of me feeling more.

Olle W: That is how it is, my friend.

Gunnar: Do you have any thoughts on this?

Olle W: You end up in a vicious cycle – you are so concentrated on how you feel, that you are not all aboard mentally, and then you become scared since you have not been mentally active. Instead, try to concentrate intensively and think in detail on what you are doing and live in the moment – mindfulness, you know.

Gunnar: I feel as if my head is so occupied by thoughts all the time, both thoughts that I am aware of and thoughts that are unconsciously gnawing at me.

Olle W: That is right – think instead of what you see around you, and what is happening outside of you. I suspect that when you get frightened because you are not keeping up, you try to clarify this by analyzing and pondering over how that happened, and if you have done something that you were not aware of. This is thinking comforting thoughts, which makes you even more frightened of your not being able to concentrate the following times. I wish that you could be present in the moment (and not think about your thoughts and that you do not remember, or do not know how this or that happened). Direct your attention to things outside yourself, and not towards your thoughts.

Gunnar: I am often frightened when I do things and then, in hindsight, I start thinking; how come I did that/said that? I had not planned on doing/saying that?

Olle W: You are looking for explanations. Comforting thoughts, comforting thoughts and once again, comforting thoughts.

Gunnar: I suppose that most people do things without thinking ahead about them, but to me, it has become a trigger for instant worry.

Olle W: That is right. Comforting thoughts are an escape from discomforting thoughts, which make these triggers. Do not be afraid of looking at your discomforting thoughts when they appear. You will not like them, but endure them when they come, and do not actively try to get rid of them. Let them come and go as they please.

Gunnar: I get frightened when I have not been actively conscious in my choices of what to do and say. Of course, this creates a lot of anxiety, when you do things without "making decisions".

Olle W: You are making things harder for yourself. Thinking about this and trying to solve this becomes comforting thoughts.

Gunnar: If I go and wash my plate after I have eaten, it is nothing that I plan to do, you just do this – out of old habits – but this has now become a trigger.

Olle W: You have tried to sort out why and how. This has now turned into comforting thoughts. It means that you have escaped from this uncertainty, so the uncertainty has now become a trigger for you. You have become frightened of things

That other people do and experience 1000 times per day.

Gunnar: I am very frightened that I have not been actively conscious of things that I have done.

Olle W: So what? Instead, try to be intensely present in the moment, the situation, the act from the beginning. Do not care about things that have passed. We cannot, and should not remember everything, instead we should save our memory's capacity and our consciousness for upcoming surprises and real dangers.

Gunnar: It can almost feel as if I am first sitting down and eating, and then everything goes black and then, all of a sudden, I have washed my plate and put it in the dishwasher. Everything in between, getting up from the chair, getting to the dishwasher, washing and putting the plate in the dishwasher, I just did without thinking.

Olle W: So what? Just state that this is the way it is. Do not try to remember everything, or how everything has happened.

Gunnar: I probably have so many thoughts about my thoughts during that process that the feeling of not knowing is reinforced. Alternatively, the stress that is constantly in my head makes me absent-minded.

Olle W: Do not look for the reason, because this will only lead to a lot of discomforting thoughts, since you are doing this to decrease anxiety. It is thinking comforting thoughts, which stimulates further discomforting thoughts.

Gunnar: This was just one example. I can also feel unpleasant when I am talking. "Did I decide to say what I said?"

Olle W: You do not decide in advance what to say, you speak when you get the notion and when you know what to reply. You take the chance and say what you think that you want to say.

Appendix C

Gunnar: Or when I go someplace; "Why did I go here, did I decide on going here?"

Olle W: Look at what happens with an interest and perhaps fascination, but do not analyze, because that will turn into comforting thoughts, which will only frighten you and turn your discomforting thoughts into triggers.

Gunnar: This unpleasantness in turn creates other thoughts; what if I am demented, what if I have a tumor, what if I am going crazy?

Olle W: Exactly – comforting thoughts create more, and new discomforting thoughts.

Gunnar: These thoughts cause me to constantly have some unpleasant thought in my mind, and make me constantly feel uneasy and tense.

Olle W: Accept this and do not do anything to escape it – learn to appreciate it – suffer in silence and do not assess your thoughts. Look at the discomforting thoughts with curiosity, but do not care about where they come from or why.

Gunnar: I try to do what I have learned, but my head is constantly so occupied that I feel so much stress and I hardly know where to go.

Olle W: Occupy your head with what happens in the present and its everyday activities and what is currently at hand.

Gunnar: Even the moments when I believe that I do not have any thoughts, I feel the stress in my head. Either it is because I gnaw on thoughts to and fro without being aware of it, or because it takes time for stress and tensions to disappear?

Olle W: Here we are again. You are looking for explanations again – comforting thoughts.

Gunnar: Even if the unpleasantness of constantly feeling as if my head is stuffed with things that cause me stress creates unpleasantness. It feels as if it can easily turn into a vicious cycle that will be difficult to break.

Olle W: You should not actively break the cycle. If you do not pay it any mind, you will eventually fall out of it. This will happen once you have forgotten to notice it, and no longer care about it.

Gunnar: What I am doing wrong is ruminating and brooding too much on my discomforting thoughts.

Olle W: Correct. Yes, accept them as if they were a movie playing in front of you. State that that thought looked like that, and I have not had that thought before, but this thought was new. Or look at your thoughts the way you look at birds, flying over your head. We are so used to some birds that we do not notice them.

Sometimes, there will be a new and rare bird. It awakens our interest, but we do not ask ourselves where it comes from or why it came at this exact time. Treat your unpleasant thoughts in the same way.

Gunnar: Why do I not know why it feels unpleasant? Maybe I am sick? Why does my head feel like this? I should find out if I have a tumor.

Olle W: Now, here are a few "birds" – let them fly on by or let them circle for a while. Your frightened brain keeps making up new thoughts, it does not mean that they are all important or true. If you keep up in this manner, you will only have more anxiety.

Gunnar: Why can I never feel calm?

Olle W: Because you do not dare to leave your discomforting thoughts unattended, without giving them some "importance". You act as if your brain is telling the truth, every time it gives you a thought filled with danger. You are behaving as if all "birds" are dangerous.

Gunnar: Even when I believe that I do not have any thoughts, I feel worried?

Olle W: Your autonomous nervous system never gets the chance to sink into relaxation response, since you are trying too hard to lower your levels of concern. Calm and ease come with accepting things for what they are. We all have worries (sympaticus), and sometimes it is referred to as "stress". Stress is sometimes necessary for us to perform better – healthy sympaticus.

Gunnar: What is gnawing at me?

Olle W: Do not attempt to answer that question, you will only create more ruminations and increase your suffering. There is no way to create certainty from ruminating.

Appendix C

Gunnar: To feel so occupied by thoughts and unpleasantness that never lets go creates an almost claustrophobic feeling. You do not want anything other than being able to relax.

Olle W: Now you are doing things wrong again, by constantly striving for "feeling good". Do not forget that you must accept that you feel bad, in order for you to feel better in the long term. You cannot control your autonomous nervous system, so give up in your efforts to feel good as soon as possible. It always fails and sustains and increases your discomforting thoughts and your feeling bad.

Gunnar: Thank you for your last reply. I hope that your summer has been nice so far. I only wanted to give you a small update. In short, the anxiety and the compulsion has worked relatively well, however, it is still hard to deal with feeling absentminded and the feeling of not having control over things and my forgetfulness.

Olle W: As you have previously heard so many times. The faster you can accept (genuinely accept) your worries and not being in control, the faster you will feel better. If you are looking for feeling better, then it is a sign that you do not genuinely accept this, and that you are giving in to comfort thoughts and other safety behaviors.

Gunnar: I am having a lot of thoughts about becoming demented and having a tumor.

Olle W: Discomforting thoughts that should only be noted with acceptance and very little interest.

Gunnar: I never feel completely relaxed in my head. I do not know if it might be because of drawn-out stress, something that maybe I should not be thinking that much about either.

Olle W: On this point you are correct, but do not ponder on why, since that will once again turn into ruminating. You do not ponder on meaningless things, and that is why you forget them.

Gunnar: Like I said, there are plenty of thoughts left, but I try not to spend too

Appendix C

much time on them, (which is hard as they keep appearing).

Olle W: Let them come. Let them live their own lives. The more comforting thoughts and attempts to understand discomforting thoughts, the more discomforting thoughts and bad feelings.

Gunnar: It is hard to let go of a worry that you do not know where it comes from.

Olle W: I have explained how conditioning works and that words/thoughts, and even fragments of thoughts can turn into triggers for reactions (sympaticus) in the body. Let go of the worry by accepting it – it is wrong to care about it.

Gunnar: You often get thoughts like; "It is probably better to take this up with a doctor than letting everything be and risk dying just because you are supposed to be a good OCD-patient and not get insurances."

Olle W: Dare to take the chance that your discomforting thoughts are not true.

Gunnar: I am fighting on, and I hope that things will turn soon.

Olle W: Do not hope for things to turn, let things take the time they need. As soon as you are genuinely accepting of thinking the way you do and feel the way you do, you will feel better. But do not look for things to just turn. Let it come when it hopefully comes.

Gunnar: I keep fighting the compulsions. However I still have a lot of thoughts. I can tell you more about that when we see each other or in a later e-mail, as I am tired after a long day. I can tell you about a thing that happened during the summer. I had a tough experience at work, when I thought that I was choking on something. In hindsight, I can look back at the positive aspects of the event. I had a hard time (I have had worse many times) but this time, the sympaticus-reaction was obvious (I was dizzy and so on.). I was clear-sighted enough to think during the episode that "wow, what a sympaticus-reaction". I have never before paid so much attention to this type of reaction as in that case, which I saw as something positive, that I knew my body so well. I think it was a worthwhile experience to feel the sympaticus in that way, not just feeling the unpleasant anxiety that I normally feel.

Olle W: It is good that you noticed the physical reaction; it is the first step towards accep-

tance without taking any counteractions. I believe that this experience will make you less afraid by sympaticus in the future, and that the dizziness will not be as frightening.

The important thing is how you act when you get a sympaticus reaction – that is not performing any safety behavior whatsoever – not even thinking comforting thoughts – like reasoning with yourself or thinking about why that might be. From what I understand, you did the right thing this time.

Gunnar: The last few days have been hard. I feel that it is unpleasant to feel so "lost in my head"- Here are the discomforting thoughts you asked me to write down.

My head hurts, what if I have a tumor?

I feel absentminded which creates panic

What if my worrying will never go away

The back of my head feels soft, what if it is a tumor and I will die

I feel dizzy, maybe because of lack of oxygen, I am going to die

I feel dizzy, what if it is a tumor

If I start to do more physical exercise, maybe I will become even more absentminded

My head hurts, what if it is a stroke

What if I go crazy

What if I get so depressed that I will not want to live anymore

I have a hard time remembering things, what if I am demented

It feels like something is stuck in my throat, what if I choke

Olle must have thought that it was strange that I did not know what was tough and if I am doing any safety behaviors, maybe I have some other illness than OCD

My chest hurts, what if I have a heart attack or meningitis

Am I feeling absentminded or not? How are you supposed to feel? Hard to concentrate, what if it is because of some disease

Strange feelings in my body, what if I am becoming mentally ill

What if I have schizophrenia

Tinnitus, what if I have a tumor

Appendix C

What if I come to another world where everything is the same as in this one
What if I live forever
What if I die soon
What if I will always feel heavy-headed
What if I will always feel dizzy
What if I have some illness in my head

Olle W: You must accept all these frightening thoughts. They are your thoughts, even if you do not like them or the feelings they cause. Do nothing to fight the thoughts or the discomforting feelings. Read them several times each night and think about their meaning. Take the worries and unpleasantness this causes (avoid thinking comforting thoughts), and you will get used to them.

Remember that your thoughts are thoughts, even though your body reacts to them with anxiety. We are all going to die, and there is nothing we can do to stop it. We do not know when or how it will happen, we just know that we eventually will die. The important thing is that you expose yourself to, and dare to think the frightening thoughts, otherwise you will just become more frightened of them. You must do nothing to disprove or investigate them in any attempt to stop the thoughts. Thoughts and anxiety are a natural part of life, and it is the thoughts that make us human. Dogs and cats live in the moment and they are not even aware of the fact that they are going to die. You must take the bad with the good – it is after all an advantage to be able to perform abstract thinking – that is thinking about the future and things that are not directly in front of you. Death is not there in front of you, but it is an unavoidable event that we think a lot about.

Just accept that you are human.

Gunnar: The last few days have been tough and I keep getting new thoughts constantly.

Olle W: Accept it, even though it saddens me to hear that you are having a rough period. It must be because you keep using some form of safety behaviors (comforting thoughts), otherwise your brain would no longer be producing as many discomforting thoughts.

You are not relaxed in your approach to your discomforting thoughts. It is impossible to have a relaxed approach to something for a while, without getting used to it. It is human nature to learn from experience, and if you spend time with a bad odor (without doing anything to get rid of it), for example, you get used to it and will not sense it, even though it is still there. The same thing goes for frightening thoughts – if you let them exist, and do nothing to get rid of them – then you will get used to them and they cease to be meaningful. Just like the odor, they will still be there, but you will not sense it anymore. I wonder what you are doing to get rid of, or to fight, understand, clarify or disprove your discomforting thoughts.

Think about the discomforting thoughts as you would think of birds.

Gunnar: Among other things, I can sit around thinking about something, and afterwards I get a thought: "Did I decide on thinking that?"

Olle W: That is a "bird". Look at it, but do not think about from where or why it came.

Gunnar: But you never decide on what to think about, and matters like this one are of a more philosophical nature, but it caused so much anxiety yesterday.

Olle W: This looks like a comforting thought. What use is it to create clarity in this? Sorting this out will only result in a number of comforting thoughts that create more discomforting thoughts and more anxiety. It seems as if you did the wrong thing when you were thinking about this. Stop caring about your frightening thoughts. Look at them as birds flying through your head. Accept them.

Gunnar: I do not know how to get through the day, things keep getting worse all the time.

Olle W: Do not pay any attention to your feeling bad, never mind the comings and goings of discomforting thoughts. Do it now, for your own sake. Do it wholeheartedly. It is the key to getting rid of the problem in the long run. There are no shortcuts. Those who go for the shortcuts are thinking comforting thoughts, which lead to more discomfort and anxiety.

Gunnar: Things are okay in the mornings, but then all the small things accumulate and things get increasingly worse during the day. It feels as if I am sitting here, thinking myself crazy, if that is possible.

GLOSSARY

Who am I?
What am I doing here?

Olle W: Talk about thinking comforting thoughts! You keep spending your days checking on how you think and feel – then will it be possible to forget and get rid of the comforting thoughts? When the day is done, you have had time to think thousands of comforting thoughts, and that is why you feel worse.

Gunnar: I feel that I need a few weeks of intense training with my compulsions right now.

Olle W: The training is then to not do anything about "feeling bad". Just suffer in silence and accept it.

Gunnar: Perhaps I need some active training. Unfortunately there are hardly any compulsive behaviors, only thoughts.

Olle W: Now try to do some intensive training in not caring about whatever pops into your mind or how bad you are feeling. Exercise nonchalance in the face of whatever will appear – horrible thoughts, anxiety, feeling bad or whatever. Exercise in not caring about how you feel. Do what you need to do – be present in the tasks and situations that you are in. That is the right form of training.

GLOSSARY

Autonomous behavior

See emotional-behavior below.

Behavior chain

A chain of behaviors where the reinforcement of one behavior (a positive consequence) becomes a starter (starting stimulus) for the next behavior. And that behavior's reinforcement becomes the starter for the next behavior, and so on.

Cognition, cognitions

Thought behavior. Behaviors carried out by the brain. Similar to external, motoric behaviors in that they are learned and controllable through will.

Comforting thought

A thought with contents that temporarily provide some calm, happiness or satisfaction. The feeling can be very small and barely noticeable, but reinforcing just as well. Comforting thoughts are used in ruminations as a counter-thought to discomforting thoughts.

Conditioning

The learning of an automatic emotional reaction. When conditioning has occurred, feelings react automatically and with no regard to logic and reason. For example, through conditioning, you can get scared by something that has previously been completely neutral.

Conditioned stimulus

An object, situation or something else that through learning conditioning has received the automatic ability to cause a feeling. An example of a conditioned stimulus is a "spider", because it causes anxiety in someone with arachnophobia, or a "decision situation" that causes decision-anxiety.

Discomforting thought

All thoughts that cause discomfort, fear, anxiety, worries, anger or unpleasantness of any kind and which are fought with counter-thoughts (comforting thoughts) during ruminations.

Defusion

A way of holding on to the discomforting thought and at the same time, disconnecting it from its frightening contents and from the reaction in the body – the sympaticus reaction and the reality, through seeing it for what it really is – as nothing more than a thought.

Emotional behavior

Also called affective or autonomous behaviors. Behaviors that cannot be controlled by will and which are run by the autonomous nervous system. For example, heartbeats, sweating, the behaviors of the stomach and intestines, and so on. In this context these are the behaviors – the sympaticus reaction – that is a part of anxiety/concern/discomfort.

Glossary

Establishing condition (circumstance/operation)
A condition that increases or decreases the power of a certain reinforcement. Hunger increases the reinforcing effect of a piece of bread – that is, it makes behaving in a way that will lead to getting a piece of bread more probable. A thought that makes avoiding anxiety more probable is an establishing condition. For example the thought: "having anxiety is bad for my heart." This thought/piece of information is an establishing condition that makes it more reinforcing to avoid things that cause anxiety.

Exposure
To expose yourself to something. In behavior therapy, this normally means placing yourself in direct contact with something (a conditioned stimulus), that causes anxiety and concern in an effort to counter-condition it. Through exposure, the automatic ability to cause anxiety in the presence of the conditioned stimuli is weakened or removed e. g. counter-conditioned.

Exposure with response prevention
You expose yourself to a conditioned stimulus and refrain from using any safety behavior (response prevention), which is necessary for counter-conditioning to occur. In rumination you refrain from comforting thoughts and expose yourself for the discomforting thoughts.

Extinction
When a behavior no longer produces any reinforcement (pleasant or expected consequence), it becomes extinct. The motivation for using behaviors that do not lead to anything disappears. We cease to carry out meaningless behaviors.

External behavior
Behaviors that are carried out by muscles and the skeleton, visible movements and observable behaviors. Also called motor behaviors. These behaviors bear great resemblance to cognitive behaviors, which are also learned and controllable by our will.

Generalization
When, for example, a person starts using a behavior at home, which has been learned in school. It really means spreading, or widening, the field of use of a behavior.

Habituation, to habituate
When you get accustomed to something for example though exposure. If you walk around in an odor for a while you will not feel it after a while. You have become habituated.

Incompatible behavior
Two behaviors are incompatible to each other, if they cannot be done at the same time. You cannot think a comforting thought and a frightening worst thought at the same time. So, these behaviors are incompatible to one another.

Reinforcement C+
Every consequence of a behavior that will lead to a continued use of that behavior or to an increase of it. You could say "motivation-increasing consequence". If I am amused and pleased by jumping a skip-rope, then I will do it again. Amused and pleased reinforces the behavior to

jump a skip-rope. The pleasant consequence can also be that you are relieved of something unpleasant or discomforting (negative reinforcement), for example, doing something to decrease anxiety. Comforting thoughts are negative reinforcers for thinking discomforting thoughts.

The reinforcement formula

Also referred to as the reinforcement paradigm. Written S-R-C, and shows the behavior's (R) connection to the situation (S) and the behavior's consequences/reinforcements (C). What precedes the behavior and what follows it. Every behavior always has a strong connection to the here and now-situation, which is described in the formula.

Reaction

Behavior in the widest sense, that is all the things that a human being (an organism) can "do". To move, think and to feel.

Safety behavior

Every behavior, visible or invisible, that decreases anxiety or discomfort. Comforting thoughts are cognitive safety behaviors, that is, thoughts that we use in order to decrease discomfort in a situation.

Stimulus

Something that precedes and contributes to starting a behavior. It starts raining (S), which makes me react (R) by unfolding my umbrella so that I will not get wet (C). (One stimulus, many stimuli).

Sympaticus reaction (sympathetic reaction)

A reaction in the autonomous nervous system in cases of strong feelings, and that cannot be controlled by willpower. The sympaticus reaction is characterized by increased pulse and blood pressure, a decreased stomach and intestinal activity, a change of the blood-flow in the body. The sympaticus reaction is a preparation for fight or flight.

The worst thought

A way to make a person not spend time thinking comforting thoughts, as these just reinforce the discomforting thoughts. Thinking the worst thought is incompatible to thinking comforting thoughts and will thus prevent using comforting thinking.

Printed in Great Britain
by Amazon